If You Leave Me, Can I Come Too?

Cynthia Heimel

If You Leave Me, Can I Come Too?

THE ATLANTIC MONTHLY PRESS
NEW YORK

Reproduced by special permission of *Playboy Magazine* (all copyright © by *Playboy Magazine*): "Sleepless in Sandusky" © 1993, "If You Leave Me, Can I Come Too?" © 1994, "No Nintendo, No G-Strings" © 1994, "How to Find the Perfect Mate" © 1994, "Networking with Wolves" © 1993, "Believing in Dog" © 1993, "I'm PC, You're a Dickhead" © 1993, "Nice Girls Don't Read Romances" © 1995, "Old Guys Amok in Hollywood" © 1994, "Guns and Poses" © 1993, "Is Female Feminine?" (originally published as "I Am Woman") © 1995, "Girls' Night Out: Why?" © 1994, "Wrong Again" (originally published as "The Shame of Male-Bashing") © 1994, "Power Envy" © 1994, "The Scare of Solohood" (originally published as "Solo Contendre") © 1995, "My Life as a Tank" © 1992, "The Chicken Goes Home to Roost" © 1994, "Fathers and Daughters: A Pop Quiz" (originally published as "Daughters and Dads: A Pop Quiz") © 1994.

Several of the other pieces originally appeared in the *Village Voice*. Reprinted with permission of the *Village Voice*.

Published simultaneously in Canada
Printed in the United States of America
FIRST EDITION

Library of Congress Cataloging-in-Publication Data

Heimel, Cynthia.
    If you leave me, can I come too? / Cynthia Heimel.
    ISBN 0-87113-603-1
    I. Title.
PN6162.H396 1995   306.7—dc20   95-10314

Design by Laura Hammond Hough

The Atlantic Monthly Press
841 Broadway
New York, NY 10003

10 9 8 7 6 5 4 3 2 1

To Lynn Ann Medlin and Merrill Markoe
(and, of course, forever and always, Tex)

Contents

Introduction

It's flu season again in my household, which means I'm lying around with a hankie stuffed in my nostrils while friends bring chicken soup and the dogs try to make me feel better by sitting on my head.

Well, all but one dog. Doc, the shy and previously abused dog from my last book, has blossomed. No longer quiet, retiring, mellow, he is now a maniac in love. The object of his heart's desire, his mad obsession and constant companion is, well, a red squeaking ball.

Here's how it goes. Doc carries his beloved everywhere, except when he puts it on my lap. I'm supposed to throw it. I don't want to. I've thrown that idiot ball five hundred times today so far. I ignore him. So he sits. I'm supposed to get all excited by this. "See how good I am? I'm sitting and everything." A piercing gaze. I ignore him. Then he ups the ante and lies down. Piercing gaze, wagging tail. I'm supposed to be rapturous. I ignore him. Then he does his most famous trick. He speaks. Yes, I taught him to speak. I thought it would be fun at parties. So he speaks and speaks and speaks until I am a single, jangled nerve. Then I pick up the ball and put it on top of the closet. Then he stares at the closet for four hours, heartbroken. Finally I give it back to him. Frenzy of excitement. Running. Jumping. Squeaking. Then he puts the ball on my lap, and we're back at the beginning of the loop.

Wait. I think I hear you wondering, "What kind of introduction is this?"

I don't know! I have the flu, goddammit, but does that stop my editor from calling at all hours of the day or night, demanding that I write an introduction? Hah. Now he says it has to be in by tomorrow or we're in "serious trouble."

So forgive me if I ramble. Forgive me, my brain is gone. (I know this because on *Jeopardy* tonight they wanted to know who was the late, lamented, most famous editor of *Vogue* magazine, and I sat stunned, my brain a sluggish swirling lump of cold oatmeal. I could not come up with Diana Vreeland!)

But, in fact, you will find dogs all over this book, and just a little, here and there, about fashion. This may be because I am still living in L.A., where people think they're dressed up if they put on socks. Walk around in L.A. in a creative little outfit with just the right muted shades and the perfect witty tailoring and people only yawn and ask you what kind of car you drive. It's very disheartening.

But I like to think there's another reason for my disinterest in clothing and my interest in dogs.

Don't you think fashion is basically *over?* That the eighties kind of ruined it by making every designer a super-superstar whose every article of clothing had to cost one zillion dollars? So that now it's all money and high stakes and perfume and the creativity is gone? I remember when I used to be able to afford Comme des Garçons. Now I can't, and I don't care; the clothes have no soul.

So dogs have replaced shopping in my life. I study them, rescue strays and find homes for those I can, and I have learned that if you study the microcosm it helps you see the macrocosm. The more I delve into the details of dogs—the way they mate, compete, submit, and pee on the floor when they're nervous—the more I understand humans. And the more I see how these smallish bundles of canine devotion are treated—the way they're so cavalierly disposed of, the way they're mistreated and overlooked and condescended to—the more I realize what an incredibly flawed species humans are. We have to spay and neuter our pets, because of the incredible overpopulation, so why not also spay and neuter our humans before the entire world is covered in asphalt?

(Ha ha, I don't mean a word of it. I'm only a humorist.)

Also, I think if I were not involved in the dog cause I would become incredibly fat, instead of simply having thighs the size of Montana. Not that there's anything wrong with this, I am not a fattist.

But have you been reading the latest statistics? It seems that most Americans are now running around with the equivalent of three Thanksgiving turkeys strapped to their bodies. We are huge.

I understand how this has happened. We have killer viruses, killer bees, killer greenhouse effects, killer decimation of rain forests, killer ethnic cleansing, killer nuclear weapons all over the nation formerly known as Russia. Every time we open our newspapers we discover new terrifying things out to kill us and over which we have no control.

We feel helpless. We need comfort. We eat many Oreos.

Not me. I read the paper, see all the terrifying things, and think, "Well, I'm doing the dog thing, somebody else take care of Sarajevo." My philosophy is, Choose your cause, then put on blinders. It's wimpy, but it works.

Although it's not working with the earthquake thing. Just today my landlady came over to declare my garbage disposal broken, and she told me that it's all over the news that the next big earthquake is imminent, and it's going to be like a 7.5.

"That's ten times the size of the Northridge earthquake, side by side," she said. I don't know exactly what she meant but I still hid under my bed for two hours after she left. I hope we are alive when you read this.

I must get out of L.A. It is horrible here. I have been madly searching for a new place to live, as you'll see.

I have finally figured out why L.A. is so toxic, besides the fact that your average L.A. resident has the discernment and moral fiber of a dust bunny.

L.A. has very little, if any, contact with reality. People build houses on stilts, for God's sake! "Oh, they're perfectly safe," idiot people say, just before a mudslide slams right into the stilts and sends the houses careening down into a canyon. Then there are other idiots out here running movie studios who, in any other city, couldn't even get work saying, "Do you want fries with that?"

This can all be explained by the theory of evolution. You remember survival of the fittest? Contrary to what many believe, Darwin wasn't talking about the toughest, the most competitive, the guy with the biggest biceps. He meant that whatever fit best within the environment would grow and prosper.

L.A. is a desert. Nothing is supposed to live out here except the odd cactus. Palms and citrus trees are transplants from another land. There is nothing indigenous to eat or drink. This is a land of impassable mountains and impossible canyons, with no way for humans to become rooted. This is where coyotes deserve to rule the world.

But some fool in the movie *Chinatown* diverted the water from hundreds of miles away and turned these stunning badlands into a theme park.

When you live where you logically shouldn't, only the illogical survives and prospers. So you get past-life therapists, women with so many face-lifts they sleep with their eyes open and scumbags with license plates that read U2ENVME.

I also have to leave because L.A. is a desert guy-wise. These men are even more problematical than New York men. I think it may have something to do with the hordes of semi-naked blond nymphets with legs up to their necks who populate every corner of L.A., waving signs that say, "Take Me Right Now!"

I am still looking for a soul mate. Preferably a veterinarian. Okay, he doesn't have to have heard of the Bonzo Dog Band, but he should go weak when listening to The Band singing "When I Paint My Masterpiece."

Also he should be a feminist. This is not easy for men these days. There is too much vitriol spewing from both sexes, hostilities are huge. There is even this big move afoot to discredit all feminists for being "victims." I can't write about this now. If I do, my head, which is a giant snot-balloon, will explode. Later you'll find a temper tantrum or two.

I will only say that women must hold fast to their strength and fairness and especially their generosity.

What else? My son has a real job finally. He has his own place and his own dog and his own surprise for you.

Okay, now I am going to take a giant nap.

How Can I Dump Him
When He Hasn't Called Me?

Sleepless in Sandusky

A lot of sleepless nights and jangled days can make you come up with pretty racy theories. I'm on a book tour. I've been in hundreds of cities and talked to thousands of people and have had almost no sleep, so okay, I'm a little strange. But I like my theories anyway.

First of all, did you know that it's not just you, but that nobody's getting laid? That hardly anybody even cares anymore?

It's bad out there. Even in Iowa, where I figured everyone had sex because what else is there to do, you can't shut anyone up about her lack of sex life and his diminishing sex drive. It's a rampant, full-blown epidemic.

So my theory is that it's a Darwinian, preservation-of-the-species thing. We know for a fact that there is such a thing as a mass unconscious which connects all humans, otherwise how could an entire country be in love with *Seinfeld* and the whole world be obsessed with Michael Jordan? Unconsciously, we are all one, and we've finally noticed that the world is top-heavy with humans, turning the planet into a wasteland.

So men and women, intent on survival, have lost the will to fuck. It's the only thing that will save us. I'm sure I'm right.

Okay, if you like that one listen to this: I think we're becoming a matriarchy. The male of the species is losing his supremacy. Don't get too nervous yet. Let's begin at the beginning.

Women are unbelievably pissed off at men these days. Even (and I hope you realize how crucial this is) stewardesses.

I was shocked. It seems to me that men are trying as never before to get along with women, to make compromises, to whisper mea culpa into women's ears.

But it doesn't matter. From Toronto to Dallas, women hate them. Last year, during my last tour, women were gritting their teeth a bit but still professing their dedication to men, still hoping they'd change so we could all get along. Not anymore. Basically, it's the old commitment thing.

"They lie, they're unreliable, they only like you until you like them back," hissed an adorable air hostess as she slipped me extra peanuts while ignoring a dozen wildly gesticulating salesmen.

"This guy tells me he loves me for days, weeks," said a reporter in Dayton, "he showers me with jewels even. I'm resisting him, but gradually I start to trust him. 'I love you too,' I tell him after he's told me he loves me a thousand times.

"The very fucking next day the fucking bastard disappears. I finally track him down and guess what he says?"

" 'I don't think I'm ready for a commitment right now. I need a little space,' " I guessed.

"Bingo," she replied.

There was even an uprising in a bookstore in Minneapolis.

"Make sure you write in *Playboy* how much we all hate men," shouted one woman. She was joined by a chorus of a dozen or so: "They suck!" "They're so stupid!" "There's no point to them!"

"So we hate men now?" I wondered.

"You betcha!" they yelled in unison.

It seems that men are "not caring, sympathetic, loving or honest," and "NOT COMMUNICATORS."

"Plus," said an ethereal blonde, "you have to always play games. You can never let them know you care or they lose interest."

"Not all men are like that," I said.

"Maybe, but most of them have that blood type," she countered.

I thought about it for days. I decided she's right. Most of you are like that. I tried to figure out why.

"The whole thing's just this enormous fuckup," said my friend Jake in Austin. "It takes a woman about six months to get comfortable sexually, to feel trusting and open, and by that time we've lost interest. Okay, calm down, not exactly lost interest, but the sight of her naked body, which used to cause mad lust, has about as much interest for us as that chair there. Romantic passion does not last. Men like the hunt."

"Aha," I said, thinking about my dogs. Just like dogs, men are hunter-gatherers, they have powerful hunting instincts embedded in their DNA. And just like dogs, men have been domesticated. There's no need to run out and slay a wildebeest anymore, food just appears magically in brown paper bags. (In humans, unlike dogs, men have the primary hunting drive, since Stone Age women spent most of their time pregnant or nursing.)

Men, like dogs, still need to satiate this compelling drive. Dogs have fuzzy squeaky things which you throw at them and they chase and pretend to kill. But you can't interest men in squeaky toys. The only hunt left for them (besides putting on orange vests and going to the woods one weekend a year) is sexual. They chase women, catch them, lose interest.

Men can't even gather much anymore, what with the economy and women turning out to be as good at gathering as anyone.

In fact, much of what defines masculinity is now useless.

Fighting is out, wars are now bad. There's nothing left to conquer besides outer space, which we can't afford. We no longer have to protect ourselves from wild animals, we have to protect wild animals from us. No more cutting down trees, even tilling the land has become problematical.

The skills needed today are feminine: Getting along, sharing, nurturing those weaker and needier than ourselves, communicating, empathizing.

Which is why women are so pissed off and men so befuddled. We know that with our special skills we should be the more powerful sex, but for years our fervent desire to get laid made us slaves to our men, who needed us to act like they were the big deals or they couldn't get it up.

But now we don't care much about sex anymore. Matriarchy is right around the corner.

Or maybe I just really need some rest.

If You Leave Me, Can I Come Too?

I'm in his kitchen, and I'm thinking, "This is good. This is the way it should be. I like him, he likes me, and I'm not nuts! I am, in fact, comfortable. A *comfortable* relationship? What a strange and wondrous departure!"

Time was when I was an obsessive. I hope you're not the kind of person who just thought, "Huh? Obsessive? What's that mean?" I hope you're nodding your head, muttering, "Oh God, the nightmare of obsession! Shoot me in the head if it ever happens again!"

He just came in and nuzzled my neck, then left again without a word. We're so mellow together we don't even have to talk much. We can just *be* with each other, reading the *New York Times* and showing each other the occasional article, watching a video, even cooking together. I don't think I've cooked since 1982, but here I am.

I figure it's going so well because *he* chose *me*. When I choose a guy I go for a crazy songwriter or something. A guy who's a massive bundle of nerve endings, who feels too much too inappropriately, and ends up dying of an overdose of the cough medicine and barbiturates that he took to dull his constant consciousness. A guy who's guaranteed to leave, one way or another.

I've spent a couple of decades trying to figure out the pathology of obsession. Not out of any kind of scholarly curiosity, but because I never again want to take the telephone into the shower with me.

I never again want to have those fantasies about how my life will be so blissful if only he'll come around the corner *right now*. I never want to read an entire mystery novel by the great Susan Conant and then realize that I haven't absorbed *one word*. I don't want to bite my fingernails until they bleed, or run to the bathroom eight times waiting for *him* to arrive.

And mostly, I don't want to hear myself. During obsession I lose all willpower. I phone up hapless friends and drone endlessly. "He said he had a cute cousin, would a guy who's really interested talk about his goddamned cousin? Do you think I should call him? Oh, did I tell you I found out where he was last Wednesday? Did you say you thought I should call him?"

My friend's ears grow numb, and I know it, but I can't stop. I talk and talk because talking about him makes me feel safer, makes me feel almost as if he's with me. The minute the subject changes, all the subterranean fear and anxiety smashes my heart. I'm on a tape loop to hell.

I just figured out what I like about calmly sautéing onions in the kitchen, knowing he's on his computer in the other room. I don't feel smaller. Usually in a relationship I feel like a small person in the presence of this gigantic *Presence*. This encompassing source of warmth and security. Now I feel just as big as he is.

Don't think for a minute that I don't know what *that's* about. A baby feels she must be near the giant, warm, milk-giving mother. Mom walks out of the room to get a paper clip, the kid feels a deep panic, she'll probably die without her all-powerful provider. Then Mom comes back and baby feels secure, even blissful.

Without the object of my obsession in my sight I feel panic, I feel powerless, I feel *erased*. When he disappears on a road trip to Minneapolis, I know that I will die. To follow my bliss means get the guy. Obsession turns me infantile.

But not anymore. I've just showed him a tape of *His Girl Friday*, my favorite movie, and he smiled at me. I feel a little foolish, trotting out gifts to lay at his feet like one of my dogs, when he just likes me for who I am. He's teaching me all about the information superhighway. Will we become a complacent, "we" sort of couple? Better than the alternative.

"Obsession," says my pal Brendan, "is putting all your shit into one basket. It's projecting every single problem in your life onto the one object who's terrified that you even know her name and telephone number. Then a month later after you've sucked that one dry, you have to find a new host, begin the body-snatching process all over again."

(That's more the male version, I think. The female, instead of finding a new host, goes into a deep depression and eats Mallomars until she pukes.)

I was the perfect candidate for becoming an obsessive maniac. A normal baby absorbs oceans of parental love. Pretty soon she becomes calm when Mom leaves the room. She transfers her security needs to maybe a blanket. Then she internalizes that love, giving herself a rock-solid infrastructure of self-confidence. When normal baby grows up, she *expects* to be loved. But if a baby never gets that parental love, she keeps aimlessly searching in all the wrong places. She turns into me.

Twenty years of shrinkage later, I've got a soupçon of inner security, I don't need to compulsively relive past misery. Twenty years of shrinkage later, I can snuggle on a sofa with a peaceful man who's in the mood for crab cakes. Twenty years later I don't need a madly verbal, funny but miserable man who's teetering on the edge of the abyss. I'm fine, I'm happy . . .

I AM SO FUCKING BORED! If I don't go home right now, I am going to stomp on this guy's head! Then maybe he'll have some kind of opinion of *His Girl Friday!*

Okay, I'm home and feeling much better, thank you. This man is so very nice, but he's as dull as a dishrag, and how am I going to tell him?

"I'm sorry, honey, maybe I don't need an addict or psychopath anymore, but my man has to want something more than crab cakes. What's that? I'm a maniac? Well, I guess that's my favorite attribute, next to my tits of course. Trust me, you've had a narrow escape."

Yeah, I know that the kind of guy I need probably has had the same brand of dank childhood I had, which is why he turned into an ultraverbal, opinionated, perverse, ironic, authority-hating creative type. And I know that this is exactly the type that runs screaming from the room at the first sign of intimacy.

So sue me.

No Nintendo, No G-Strings

*I*t was a brouhaha of major proportions. "Flowers!" ranted Cleo. "He sent me flowers for my birthday, goddamn it! You get flowers from your agent, not your boyfriend. It's bad enough he's always out of town."

"Oh, well, you know, he's a guy," said Susan.

"I gave him plenty of notice," said Cleo. "Two weeks ago I started saying, 'I want you to get me something special for my birthday. It's really important to me.' I guess I'm unrealistic, but when I opened the front door this morning I expected to see a pony."

We were in a high-toned restaurant. Cleo was surrounded by presents.

"He says he's really busy," she said, "but he spent an entire month shopping for the perfect running shoes. I left him a message on his machine telling him what a dickhead he is."

Meanwhile, back at my house, my son Brodie was on the phone with Brendan, Cleo's boyfriend.

"Did they say where they were going?" Brendan asked.

"I think it begins with a *P*," said Brodie.

"Go get the Yellow Pages. Look under 'Restaurants Where Broads Go on Their Birthdays.' "

While Cleo was ranting, Brendan was calling every *P* restaurant in the phone book. He never found us.

Cleo unwrapped a clock with a Labrador's face on it and hugged it. "See, we know how to buy presents for one another."

"At least he's a good boyfriend in other ways," said Teri.

"I hate you all for sticking up for him," said Cleo.

"I didn't stick up for you," I told Brendan later.

"You're right," he said, "I'm an asshole. All men are assholes."

"I hate when men say, 'All men are assholes,' like that's a perfectly valid excuse for bad behavior."

"Shit," he said, "that one worked for years. Okay, tell me what to do."

"Just get her something she'll like."

"What the fuck is that supposed to mean?"

There was raw panic in the man's voice. It was as if I'd asked him to compute the trajectory for a space probe. This prompted me to do a survey.

"One year Howard bought me a dress that I swear to God was a size six," said size twelve Susan. "I wore it as a blouse. Guys don't even know what a dress is. They call everything a woman wears a dress."

"He keeps buying me G-strings and cameras," said Nora. "In other words, presents for him."

"I got a Super Nintendo last year for Christmas," said Maddie. "You can't tell me there's a woman alive who gives a fuck about a Nintendo game."

One year, long ago, my husband handed me a carefully wrapped present. "You've been wanting one of these for so long," he said, beaming.

It was a shower cap.

I am drawn to the conclusion that most men, as present-givers, suck. Not all men, of course. Two-timing, womanizing rat-bastards are always giving extravagant jewelry and perfect, tasteful bibelots, usually the moment before they shred a woman's heart to pieces. But that's a whole different column. Let's focus on your basic nice guy, like Brendan.

"We live in a materialistic society," Brendan said. "We have everything that we need."

"Cut the shit, Brendan. We're not talking about things we need, we're talking about symbolic tokens of affection."

"Exactly! Something you need is at least *something*. We know how to get you *something*. But speculating on an emotional thing? How do we know that a certain kind of earring isn't going to make you kill yourself? You broads have spent your entire lives contemplating earrings. A guy who's thought about earrings a lot has spent an hour, tops."

"That is such a rationalization," said Susan. "You know men's problem? They're hunters. We're gatherers. We browse, they run in and buy the first thing they see. What they really want to do is walk in with a big bloody buck on their shoulders, plop it at our feet and say 'Merry Christmas.' "

"We just don't approve of the whole gift-giving thing in the first place," said Brodie. "We don't understand it, it's always a chore. It's much easier to get gifts for guy friends. You just get what you want for yourself and they like it, too."

"Aha!" I said. "I've just realized the root of the problem. Men, as a rule, are not empathetic. To be a good present-giver you have to turn yourself into the other person."

"Forever?" asked the smart-ass.

Yes, I told him, at least while you're in a present-buying mode. Social mores have trained women to be empathetic, to put ourselves in the other guy's shoes and care more about his feelings than our own. This is why we have boundary problems and shrink bills.

Whereas too many guys are afraid to root around in their

psyches to find some empathy, in case they stumble on something scary, such as their dreaded sensitive (a.k.a. feminine) sides. But empathy is so useful at Christmas.

When buying presents, I put myself into a little trance. I'm Brodie, I say to myself. I'm kind of jockish, a blue-eyed, left-wing kind of guy. Yo, what about that cool blue-gray shirt? Is that me, or what?

Or maybe I'm Cleo. I'm whimsical, funny. The most beloved thing in my life is my old dog. Hey, look at that clock over there!

"What I really want," said Cleo, "is for him to buy me something that acknowledges who I am. Or, of course, something from Tiffany's. The best present I ever got from Brendan was a trash can with Labrador retrievers all over it."

Actually, that shower cap wasn't so bad, either.

When the Phone Doesn't Ring,
It'll Be Him

YOU: Okay, it's been only two days, but that's too long. I think, no, *I know,* that when someone says, "Are you going to be there for a while? I'll call you right back," they should fucking well call you back. I think.

FRIEND ONE: Who called who?

YOU: He called me! You see what I mean? He called me! A day and a half after a perfectly nice date with kissing and everything. Here's the entire phone call: Chat chat chat, had a really good time the other night, joke joke joke, doorbell ring, I'll call you back, then nothing for fifty-one hours.

FRIEND ONE: Was it a peck kiss or a sex kiss?

YOU: It was a sex kiss. Not tongues though.

FRIEND ONE: But like open mouth and body pressing?

YOU: Yep.

FRIEND ONE: And you said nothing weird during the phone call? Nothing clingy, no "When am I going to see you again?" or asking questions about other women? No mentioning movies you're just dying to see?

YOU: No. Light, silly, and not even fake light silly. I was thinking "Do I really like you? Are you smart enough?" not "Do you like me? Do you really? Will you stay with me forever?" He seemed to really like me, I was feeling secure. Do you think when they seem to really like you that means they're going to disappear? Is this a new law?

FRIEND ONE: Who the hell knows what they mean. They live in an alternate universe. I say dump him. You don't need this. If he's already behaving badly, just think of the future.

YOU: How can I dump him when he hasn't called me? It's wrong to call him just to dump him, isn't it? Anyway, I'm afraid of confrontations. But if he should call me back, I'll dump him. I don't need this.

FRIEND TWO: I know what you're doing. Believe me, I know, I've done it. But just don't. Don't make rules for yourself.

YOU: I can't make rules for anyone else, that's for sure.

FRIEND TWO: Just see what you feel like when he calls you, see what he says, just take it moment by moment. Don't try to lock in future behavior.

YOU: Hey come on, this is really not a good sign!

FRIEND THREE: That's right, it isn't. And you have to pay attention. You have to find someone to treat you well, you deserve it. I thought it was a good sign that he is in the program, because he shouldn't be scared of vulnerability, but what do you know about his issues?

YOU: I don't care about his issues. His issues aren't my issues. The last thing I want to do is spend hours figuring out his motivation, analyzing him.

FRIEND THREE: Boy, if he does call you again, he'd better have a good excuse.

YOU: He just moved here, you know, and we New Yorkers eat their young. Men have to feel that they're powerful, that they're on top of things. I'm not even sure he really has a job. During our date he kept telling me these stories to impress me. I was so bored. Now, however, four days since he called, he is the most fascinating man alive. Do you think he'll call when he gets a job?

FRIEND THREE: What are you doing?

YOU: What am I doing?

FRIEND THREE: You're analyzing him. You said you weren't going to analyze him.

YOU: I want a doughnut. A sugary, chocolate-covered, cream-filled doughnut. Which would poison me. I'm not allowed sugar, I'm not allowed yeast, I'm not allowed anything deep-fried. Suicide by doughnuts.

FRIEND FOUR: I know just how you feel. He's probably one of those really passive guys who needs a mother figure, I know. He never pays for anything, he can't make decisions, he's passive-aggressive, always flirting with your girlfriends and pretending he's not . . .

YOU: He's nothing like that at all.

FRIEND FOUR: Isn't he? Roger is just like that. Did I tell you he sent me a Christmas card? So then I called him, and I know I shouldn't be with him or anything, you know, but he sounded so, I don't know, so . . . contrite? It's just a game, don't you think.

YOU: I have to go now.

FRIEND ONE: So how much weight have you gained?

YOU: Look, I thought Wednesday was the worst, I was really devastated on Wednesday. But Saturday was even worse, I'd seen him for the last two Saturdays, last night I ate at the Chelsea Gallery by myself, all these couples falling on each other. It's like a nasty joke. You're just about starving to death, somebody dangles a cheeseburger right in front of your nose, they let you have one little crumb, then they whip it away.

FRIEND ONE: Oh, fuck it, forget your pride. Call him. Just try not to beg.

YOU: Do you really think I should?

Dear Problem Lady:

What is this business with sports? Why are people so crazy? I hate to sound like a stereotype, but I am a baseball, basketball and hockey widow. Especially this year, something seems to be going on in hockey and basketball that has my husband in a real dither. One of those stupid games was on last night and I couldn't talk to him at all.

"Hon," I said, "I'm thinking of going back to school to become an antiques appraiser."

"Pick and roll!" Mitch screamed.

"No," I said, "not particularly picks or rolls, just general antiques. You know, Aubusson carpets, folk art . . ."

"Get the rebound, goddammit, Mason!" he yelled.

"I wouldn't exactly call Mason jars folk art," I said, confused.

Whereupon he accused me of chattering inanely and locked me in the bedroom.

I just don't understand how men, and also my friend Julie, can get so worked up about pituitary cases running back and forth and throwing a ball around.

And the way these sports people say "we." As in "We are ahead by ten points!" And "We won!" "We lost!"

What "we"? Why "we"? I don't see my friend Julie out there throwing some stupid ball into a basket. She just sits in her living room stuffing her face with corn chips.

It makes me have less respect for Julie. But that's not so bad, I never respected her much anyway, she wears awful shoes. But now I'm losing respect for Mitch, who usually is my darling husband, except now. Now I don't even know what he's talking about. What *is* a "pick-and-roll," anyway? And who cares?

Adrienne

Dear Adrienne:

I can understand why Mitch locked you in the bedroom. I can't understand why he didn't stuff a sock in your mouth.

It is perfectly fine not to care for or understand sports. But it's just plain lazy not to get the *point* of sports.

Are we, or are we not, a tribal species? We're constantly being tribelike in exactly the wrong instances, like hating foreigners, or gays, or weirdos with blue hair. They threaten us, they're not part of our gang.

And do we not, all of us, have a strong current of competition running through our systems? Even a mild-mannered antiques appraiser will often want to push another mild-mannered antiques appraiser over a cliff.

And this is not some neurotic twentieth-century human thing. Look at dogs, lions, apes. Tribal, competitive, constantly jockeying for position.

In the modern world, we have but few chances to act on these biological imperatives. So we either start totally inappropriate and cruel race wars or we sit in a stadium swilling beer and acting stupid. Which would you prefer?

The pick-and-roll is where one guy guards another guy so that. . . . No, it's when one offensive player throws the ball to. . . . No, that's not it either . . .

Problem Lady

Dear Problem Lady:

My boyfriend is making noises about moving in together. We've been seeing each other for four months. I think it's too soon.

But he's so cute! I haven't gone out with someone this presentable in like a decade! Clean clothes, matching socks, real job! I'm used to the scraggy carpenter-musician type! And he's a good guy with a warm heart and everything!

The thing is, he's kind of passive. Like when we go to the movies, I say, "Where do you want to sit?" and he says, "Where do *you* want to sit?" At first I thought this was charming but now I'd really like him to say, "I like to sit up close in the middle." Then I could say, "I like to sit farther back." And we could negotiate. This way I'm afraid he's just seething with annoyance wherever we sit.

Now when I say he wears clean clothes and has a good job, I don't mean some straight fuck in a suit at a bank. This guy wears jeans and cool shirts and he's an animal behaviorist. I should give all this up just because he won't tell me where he wants to sit in the movies?

Speaking of movies, he gets mad if I go without him. I went to see a film with a friend and he sulked for two days. "I thought we were going to see it *together,*" he said a few hundred times. I don't want to be one of those women whose other friends stop inviting her to things because she always has this boyfriend in tow.

He doesn't even mind if my cat sleeps in the bed. Even if that cat sleeps on his head. The cat likes him, that must mean he's a great guy, right?

I'm just worried that I might have to take care of him. His last girlfriend, Crazy Rhoda, was also his business partner and did the books and everything and he keeps hinting around that he would like me to quit my job and work with him. When he says this, my throat clutches up.

But if I say I don't want to move in with him, I'm afraid he'll break up with me and it'll be another decade before I have a decent boyfriend.

Ellen

Dear Ellen:

Looks like you've got yourself one of those merging guys. A guy who's not quite sure who he is and doesn't feel whole unless he's got a girlfriend. A guy who turns "togetherness" into an Olympic sport.

If you're not careful, he will smother you, cool shirts and all. (Speaking of smothering, have you wondered why the cat sleeps on his actual head?) Plus he'll constantly be thinking up new dramas to get you to prove that you love him.

Don't panic. You don't have to break up with him. But when he starts encroaching, when his needs and demands take up all the air in the room, stand your ground. No moving in, no quitting your job, no only going to the movies with him. You give in, he'll keep escalating until you're talking to each other solely in baby talk.

Faint heart never won fair gentleman. It's no good having a boyfriend if you lose yourself.

Problem Lady

Dear Problem Lady:

I just broke up with someone on Friday but I'm fine. I cried for a day and a half solid, and now every evening at six sharp I'm suicidal until after *Jeopardy,* when some poor sap of a friend forces herself to have dinner with me and listen to me rave for twenty-five minutes and then I'm okay again until four A.M., when I wake up and my brain turns into a war room.

First I better say there's some dispute about whether we broke up. I was convinced we were an item ever since what I considered our first date.

And I'm not a total idiot about dates. I know you can't always tell. You think a guy's interested, next thing you know he's saying, "What are you talking about? Aren't we just friends?"

But there was definitely real kissing and holding hands and bodies pressed together and I'm sorry, but that's dating, am I right? Plus there was flirting and faxing cute cartoons and constant phone calls.

So anyway, then after a really fun, hot make-out session I don't hear from him for an abnormally long three days and I'm getting that familiar sinking feeling thinking, "Ohfuckohfuckohfuckohfuck," but then I'm thinking, "Nah, we're having too good a time," and then finally he calls and says he just has to tell me he's not available for a romantic sexual relationship and he's seeing too many other people. So I say what were you doing with me then? So he said he didn't know for sure where things were going with me until the hot, fun make-out session. And kind of acted as if I were nuts or something. He even got a little hostile at one point. And I said thank you very much I'll be crying for days now good-bye.

So of course my brain, which is a female brain, remembers every salient detail of every conversation, not to mention every touch, every overheard remark, every fax, every glance. And so at four in the morning, my eyes pop open like a demented puppet, and suddenly it's like NASA in my head,* hundreds of people staring at computer screens—making graphs and pie charts, collating and cross-referencing information, plotting, assembling statistics and computing probabilities, shouting "Defcon three!" and using the red phone to call the commander in chief.

And after three days of this frantic nocturnal computing I have come up with my answer: The guy is fucking nuts.

And that's all there is to it.

But not to my girlfriends.

Naturally the phone has been surgically attached to my ear since the unfortunate event, one must have support.

But must they keep talking about his relationship with his mother? Must they keep referring me to one of those insufferable books like *Men Who Hate Women and the Women Who Make Foolish Choices and Also Love Too Much*? Must they incessantly draw parallels between my current tragedy and their last disaster?

Metaphor courtesy of Steven Wright.

They are analyzing this guy to death. They are asking me his sign and doing astrological charts. They are speculating about his intimacy issues.

And I just can't stand it. Who gives a fuck what this guy's story is? Who *cares* about his motives? Not me. All I care about is getting him out of my head as soon as possible. And when my gal pals get all analytical I get all anxious, panicky and pissed off because they're putting him right back in my head and it's horrible. I miss him.

Although I am fine. Not so fine on Valentine's day. But fine now.

Two questions: Why are my friends doing this? And why does it bother me so much?

Keesha

Dear Keesha:

Two things:

1) You are not fine. You're still in shock. Don't be surprised if the waves of misery continue for a while. They'll go away soon enough because

2) You are disgustingly healthy. It's almost nauseating the way your sense of self has remained intact.

You know why your friends have gone into instant analysis mode? Because that's what they do when they're heartbroken. And the reason they do it is that they secretly think it's their fault.

Women are born (or rather, raised) to take the blame. We've had it pounded into our collective heads that we're supposed to make everything okay, make everyone like us, make men happy. And if we don't, we're fucked up.

So we analyze, rationalize, come up with arcane, ornate theories simply to run away from the horrible little voices in our heads saying, "You should have been prettier! Nicer! Not so demanding and needy, you schmuck!"

You're not doing this. Give yourself a pat on your own back

for understanding what's going on, that you got involved with a hostile weirdo.

Too bad understanding is the booby prize.

Problem Lady

The Hidden Life of Women Who
Run with the Dogs

How to Find
the Perfect Mate

*L*ots of you know me as a lone, hard-bitten columnist, prone to lurking on deserted rocky promontories while searching for my muse.

But did you know that I also have another life as a match-maker? I swear. Every day I go to work and become a yenta, trying to bring together lonely souls desperate for love.

Okay, it's true that half of these souls are orphaned dogs in a rescue kennel, which is somewhat different from a person you want to have sex with. But not that different. There are still the love and commitment factors, the boundary problems, the weeding out of abusive or withholding or just generally lousy humans who want dogs for all the wrong reasons. Like for target practice, or lab research.

I've gotten pretty good at it. I can tell a softhearted, sappy human who will let his dog sleep under the covers from the flakes and fuckheads in approximately ten minutes. And now I'm going to apply the same principles to my love life.

I used to sit up and beg, roll over, fetch and play dead for any guy who showed the vaguest interest in me. I would trot right along home with him and try not to notice that we were eating Brand X kibble and that he kept trying to get me to play in traffic. But now I have a new leash on life. Now I will withhold judgment. I will ask many questions.

These questions will be deceptively casual and nonleading. You don't ask a prospective owner, "Will you let your dog sleep on the bed if she wants to?" because he'll say, "Why, of course!" just to shut you up. No, you ask, "Where will the dog sleep?" If the prospective says, "Out in the yard, or maybe in the garage if she's lucky," instead of, "Wherever she wants," this is a person who has no interest in the comfort or feelings of a longtime companion. This person does not get a dog.

I guess the "Where will I sleep?" thing won't work with a lover, but there are ways to gauge compassion and empathy in a mate. At some point during the early part of a relationship, the guy doesn't call when he says he will. It's a guy rule, just as it's a woman rule to say she'll be home when he calls and then purposely isn't. These are courtship rituals to see how much we can get away with.

When the guy didn't call, I used to pretend nothing had happened. Such behavior sets the relationship back to square one, with everyone pretending to be madly casual. Other people will tearfully cry, "Where the hell were you?" which is leading and demanding and pushes the relationship too far forward.

Here's what I'll do: I'll ask blandly, "How come you didn't call on Thursday?" If I get, "Oh, was I supposed to call?" I won't mind. Nobody likes to admit he's playing games. Although, now that the guy has been warned, if he does it again, he doesn't get the dog.

But if he has a hissy fit about how you can't tie him down and he was just too busy and what's the big deal anyway, I will run away. This guy is way too defensive, his ego is too fragile, he has too much fear of getting close.

I always ask a prospective owner, "Have you had dogs

before?" If she answers, "Hey, yeah, lots and lots." I keep up the questions. If Scruffy got hit by a car, and Fido just ran off one day, and she gave Rover to a friend because Rover chewed up the sofa, there is no way in hell I'll even finish the conversation. I want people who stick with their dogs through anything, people whose dogs live to be fifteen.

Again, I can't expect a guy to keep all his girlfriends until they die. In fact, if he did I'd be mega-concerned. But history is important. If Madge was a real bitch who took him for all he was worth, and Heather was a total basket case who just used him and abused him, and Fiona, well, she was one crazy lady—he wouldn't be surprised if she were a drug addict or worse—then I'll hide under the house until this guy leaves.

Because we know it takes two to tango. One person is never insane and the other lovely and sweet. A man is allowed one harridan in his early twenties, but then he must admit to equal responsibility. There is nothing more dangerous than someone who thinks of himself as a victim. Victims feel it's within their rights to fuck over everyone.

Sometimes people call hysterically, saying they want a dog right away because their dog died yesterday. No dog I show them fits their requirements, since they are looking for the dog they just lost. Dog-bereaved people have to wait a few months. The relationship-bereaved must wait even longer: Shrinks say it takes half as long as the relationship lasted to get over it. I will not go for a guy who is awash with feelings, negative or positive, for another woman.

Then there are the people who desperately want a dog, but they're unemployed and rent a furnished room in a house with no fenced yard. If they can hardly take care of themselves, they should know better than to think they can spring for dog food and vet bills.

Likewise, plenty of guys tell you all over the place how desperate they are for a woman, and then you visit them and there's a mountain of unpaid bills on the table and penicillin growing in the refrigerator. I already am a mother.

And then there are the weird ones. People who say all the right things, but somehow I get a bad feeling in the pit of my stomach. Or people who seem so lovely that when they say something like, "We already have two cats, but we wouldn't mind if they got lost," I try to pretend I didn't hear that glaring callousness, because I'm so desperate to get the dog out of a kennel and into a home.

But then I realize the kennel's fine for now. Nobody should be so desperate that they ignore big red flags thrown right in their faces.

Networking with Wolves

I don't pretend to be a soothsayer, but I know what the big self-help wave of the nineties will be about.

We are all suddenly going to remember that we, too, are animals. That we used to have these wild instincts that had nothing to do with television or Stair Masters. That these instincts still lie dormant within us, and if we want to lead lives that have meaning, we must find our animal selves, the part of us still connected to the Earth.

How do I know this? Because it's true and because it's already starting.

Haven't most of us become tree-huggers? Hasn't the idea that the Earth is on a straight sure path to destruction traveled deep into our mass consciousness? Don't we all have towers of old newspapers in our hallways that we will take to the recycling center someday really soon? Have we not gone back to cloth diapers, or do we not feel guilty every time we buy Huggies? Have we not elected Al Gore?

And hasn't the animal rights movement become so big that it scares the old establishment to the point where that dowager duchess of a TV show, *60 Minutes*, feels compelled to take a stand? (There was a military scientist who, if I have it right, was cutting up cats to study head wounds. Many animal lovers were rather upset. And *60 Minutes* implied they had no right to be. I hope its ratings plunge into hell.)

A major player in this back-to-nature motif is the wolf. He used to be a big, bad guy. Now he wears a white hat. Now we decry ranchers who shoot wolves. The wolf is a symbol of freedom, instinct, wildness. The wolf is our new superstar. We had *Dances with Wolves*, now we have *Women Who Run with the Wolves*, a book by Clarissa Pinkola Estés, which has been at the top of the best-seller lists for weeks.

Every woman I know has bought this book. The title cried out to our secret longings. Every secretary, every waitress, every dry-cleaning clerk in the world is dying to chew up her steno pad or receipt book, grow a tail and fangs, and make a run for it. We want to go wild, have fantastic adventures, lick our genitals and howl. When the boss asks us to bring him coffee, we want to snarl and go for his throat.

Unfortunately, it's kind of a lame book. An *Iron John* for women—a hodgepodge of myths, symbolism and preaching. You read it, looking for a way to break out of your stultifying life, and the author tells you to stop whining and break out of your stultifying life. Just do it, she says. And when you ask, "How? How? Oh, please, how?" she trots out a pretty tale about Jungian archetypes. Her only tangible advice is to get your hands muddy whenever possible.

I was so disappointed. I wanted blood, guts, sex. I wanted to scramble around at the bottom of my reptilian brain. I got clichéd poetry and prissiness. The chapter on sex was the worst. It was the shortest chapter in the book and was entirely about how a dirty joke, when told by a politically correct mythological goddess, can have healing powers. There was one about a runaway penis. Don't ask.

Come on, Clarissa Pinkola Estés. Shouldn't sex be the meatiest chapter? Isn't the biggest problem facing men and women the fact that our instincts are buried under centuries of civilized morality, under a crushing weight of neurosis and guilt? We have no idea how we feel about one another, or even how to speak to one another without growing hostile. Don't we need to bring those buried instincts into the light? Wolves are monogamous and mutually supportive—tell us about that.

Okay, maybe disappointment has made me harsh. There are some good moments. Her words are moving when it comes to bodies. "We tend to think of body as this 'other.' Many people treat their bodies as if the body were a slave. Perhaps they even treat it well but demand it follow their wishes and whims as though it were a slave nonetheless," she says. "Do we wish to spend a lifetime allowing others to detract from our bodies, judge them, find them wanting?"

No, we don't! Throughout their lives, women try to pummel their bodies into some phantom ideal shape that exists only with a lot of airbrushing. If we could just exhale, let ourselves be fat or thin and stop implanting and liposucking, we'd begin to feel free, sexy, alive. (I don't blame men for this. Men seem to go for us no matter what size and shape we are. I blame capitalism. No, really. The consumer must constantly be in a state of anxious low self-esteem so that she will constantly buy lipsticks and girdles to make her feel cuter.)

I also learned something about relationships. Estés says that when you start noticing imperfections in your mate, when every cell in your body tells you to run away, that's when you should stay. I like this. She also talks about how many men are wounded, hate themselves for it and deny that it is true. Such a man looks outside himself for something to heal him, but nothing ever does. The only things that will save him are admitting and having compassion for his wounded state.

This sounds right to me. If men could stop hating themselves and holding in their pain, maybe they would stop being so rigid and judgmental and unhappy. Maybe they would like women better.

But these insights are not enough for more than four hundred pages of rambling. *Women Who Run with the Wolves* is a best-seller only because of its killer title.

I've learned a hell of a lot more about why we do what we do by reading dog books: Dominant and submissive behaviors, pack psychology, eye contact, territorialism, sexual jealousy, it's all there.

Last night I dreamed that I was chasing a pack of wolves, trying to belong. They looked back at me and asked, "Who is that and why is she wearing panty hose?"

Believing in Dog

I'm thinking about getting myself an old guy. An old guy won't be so much trouble. He'll lie around on the couch, eat, fart, scratch, sleep. Young guys run around too much, need too much attention and are constantly picking fights.

Plus, nobody wants old guys. People want puppies—cute little bits of fur that pee on your bed and eat your sofa. But well-mannered old guys, four or five or even twelve years old, guys who would never lift a leg in the house, guys who find shoe-chewing boring and passé, are passed over. They languish in kennels, they are gassed at animal shelters.

I have a newspaper on my coffee table called *Muttmatchers Messenger*—pages and pages of pictures of pooches for adoption. Most morons who abandon their dogs do it when the animals are about a year old, when they're no longer cute little puppies but they're still gnawing on table legs because nobody bothered to teach them not to. But in this paper there is a picture of a ten-year-old guy who was abandoned at a market. A man drove up to the market, dropped off the old dog and drove away. The old dog waited for him in front of the market for a week. Some kind woman finally rescued him. Now this faithful old guy is just waiting in a kennel. I've been looking at his picture for eight months.

Too many people are stupid about dogs. Too many people want purebreds, because purebreds with AKC papers supposedly have status. But kennel clubs are dog destructive. They hold these beauty contests called dog shows. The dogs have no job but to look pretty. So irresponsible breeders find one pretty dog and breed it over and over to its sisters, its daughters. Purebred dogs are now riddled with health problems and are incapable of doing the jobs they were bred for in the first place.

And where does your average human go for his purebred dog? To the mall, where the pet stores sell puppy-mill dogs at inflated prices. Puppy-mill dogs are so unhealthy that half of them die. Puppy-mill owners keep dogs in tiny cages where they become deranged and catatonic.

This morning I couldn't stand it anymore and phoned about the old guy.

"Yes," said the dog-rescue woman, "poor old Homer's still here."

"Is he doing okay?"

"Most of our dogs are relatively happy. They'd rather have homes, but they're okay. Homer just sits and waits."

Oh God, I can't do this. My other dogs will kill me. Most of the men I know have one dog with whom they bond intensely, put red bandannas on and take everywhere. An us-against-the-world kind of thing. Most women I know have two or even more dogs with whom they construct close-knit family units. I have no idea what this means.

But I do know that having a dog makes us happier. Dogs and humans are symbiotic species. We need each other. A dog is the only animal that has a love of humans embedded in its DNA. This has been true for thousands of years.

My dogs protect me from homicidal gardeners, from psycho

mailmen. They really scare the shit out of prowling Jehovah's Witnesses. They accompany me to the bathroom in the middle of the night in case something scary is lurking.

With dogs, you don't need gurus. Dogs are forever in the moment. They are always a tidal wave of feelings, and every feeling is some variant of love. They take us out of our heads and into our lives. They remind us of where we came from.

Dogs, the poor slobs, hand over their entire lives the way we hand someone a tissue. And in turn we kill them. In this country, eight million animals die every year at animal shelters.

I know I'm a castrating bitch, but, fellows, you have to cut your dog's balls off. Dog and cat overpopulation is at a point where we can't let our dogs randomly reproduce. Yes, your dog is the cutest, smartest dog in the world and you just have to have one of his pups, but I'm sorry, you can't. There are just so many dog owners to go around, so every time you bring a new puppy into the world you're sentencing another dog to death.

I know you're wincing and grabbing at your own balls in a frenzy of projection, but get over it. I have two neutered guys. They are not fat or lazy. They are playful guys who don't have to go through the frustration of always wanting it and rarely, if ever, getting it. They fight less, roam less; they bond better and are more protective. Plus, a neutered dog has a 98 percent reduction in cancer and infection and will live an average of two years longer than a guy with balls. (You also have to spay your females. But most men, go figure, have no trouble with this concept.)

I had two neutered guys when I wrote that last paragraph. Now I have three neutered guys. Homer is right over there on the couch.

He's been in a constant state of amazement since I got him. He was, as promised, just sitting there in his kennel while a bunch of young guys frolicked around him. He saw my leash and couldn't believe it was for him. He was all, "Me? Are you sure? Really? Oh boy!" He put his paws around my neck and licked my face. In the car he was beside himself with wriggles. Then the couch situation put him in a state of shock.

"Are you telling me I'm allowed up here? Is this a joke? Can I roll around and everything?"

He is an extremely well-behaved guy. Most rescued dogs are. They're so grateful to have a home.

Don't buy a dog. Go to the pound. Or to a rescue group, which probably runs classified ads in your local paper. If you're a breed snob, you can find golden retrievers, cocker spaniels, anything.

Or get an old mixed breed like Homer, who's now running and yipping in his sleep, probably dreaming of runaway mailmen.

The Hidden Life of Women Who Run with the Dogs

8:11 A.M.: I am awakened by the feeling of many tongues on my face. Some tongues snake into my nostrils, some vigorously clean my ears. I feel a large paw on my head. I open my eyes warily. It is only the dogs. "Wake up, wake up!" they all cry. "Wake up and let's go to the cupboard of the kitchen where you keep the chopped dead animal!"

I consider going back to sleep, but they have been peeing on the carpet lately in their wildish way. I sit up in bed. Pandemonium ensues. "Yes, yes!" they all cry. "You are awake! This is the most fabulous thing that has ever happened in the history of time!"

"You really love me, don't you?" I coo as I lead them into the yard. (You may wonder at my fluency in dog language. I took a course in Wicca at the nail salon on Sixteenth Street. Suddenly the mysteries of the canine kingdom were unlocked before me.)

"Love you?" They look puzzled. "What makes you think so?"

"You lick my face incessantly. You push each other out of the way to get to my nostrils."

"You are our new mother," they say. "When we were puppies we licked our mother's face and she would vomit up food for us.

When we lick your face you go to the magick cupboard. You keep us infantilized. If you'd only let us hunt with you we would grow up." This is an old argument.

2 P.M.: We're in the garden, communing, reminding ourselves of the life/death/life cycles of nature, our wildish mother: spring, summer, autumn, winter. In Los Angeles it is fire, floods, earthquakes, riots in a never-ending panoply.

The calla lilies are in bloom again. We sit for another hour. A feeling that has no name overtakes me.

"What is this feeling?" I ask Sally, my small familiar.

"Boredom," she snaps without hesitation. "Who wants to sit for hours staring at a bunch of plants?"

"Yeah," says Mike, Sally's husband. "Fuck this, let's eat again. Let's kill something. Let's sniff somebody's butt."

Sally and Mike are in mad, romantic love. Over the years they've had 40 puppies, who in turn have had 800 puppies, who in turn have had 16,000 puppies, who in turn have had 320,000 puppies.* All from my little two! Some would say that letting so many puppies enter the world when three-fourths of all puppies die before they are a year old is cruel and irresponsible. Is it my fault that not enough people want to commune and feed and pay the vet bills for seven dogs? How could I thwart Sally and Mike's natural spirit by neutering them?

Sometimes the other dogs kill and eat Sally's puppies. Then they seem oddly guilty.

I dig some earth and let it run through my fingers to harken back to my true self and assuage the anxiety of my last thought. That doesn't work, so I take some Valium.

---

*For the very literal-minded reader, my dogs are all spayed and neutered and are always on a leash.

7 P.M.: "Hunt, hunt, hunt!" the dogs chant. Ever since a woman at Wicca class told me to let my dogs run wild and free because she read about it in some best-selling book my dogs have been after me.

I open the door, they charge through. I jump on my bicycle and speed after them, ready for some mystical experience, ready for an alternate canine universe to become manifest.

They sniff bushes. One pees, the other pees on top of that pee, the first one pees on top of that pee. They try to engage other dogs on the block, but all the dogs are behind fences or windows, held back by their less-enlightened humans.

Suddenly the dogs take off toward downtown. I follow at breakneck speed. We come to a neighborhood teeming with loose dogs. My dogs find a wild pack. They circle them. The wildish dogs circle back. My dogs circle again. Except the tiny ones, who hide behind my ankles. Then my dogs find another pack and circle again. I wonder why I don't find this wondrous. I wonder why the dogs on the street look at me beseechingly and ask me to take them home so they can stop circling with all these suburbanites and lie on a nice sofa and have a decent meal.

I wonder at my dogs' amazing facility to circumvent traffic. Just then a wildish Mack truck comes careening around the corner and mows them down.

10:32 P.M.: "That will be $10,000, and I'm still not sure we can save the little one's leg," says the emergency veterinarian.

I pant and run in circles, chasing my tail.

Now We Are Eight

I'd like to write a column, it's my dearest wish, and I'll really try, but things are out of control . . .

Editor's note: This is true. This column was days late.

Wherever I go, whatever I do, there are noses. There are bodies and tails and paws. There is a continuous cacophony of barking, snuffling, panting and chewing. There is the incessant threat of eye contact.

Six pairs of doggy eyes try to gaze at me every minute of the day. I used to be so flattered, I thought I was being adored, kind of a dog shrine, but if you read enough dog books, you find out that dogs use eye contact to play chicken. If you look away first, you're being submissive and they decide they're the pack leader, run amok and eat your curtains.

So I spend too many hours of the day staring them down. And throwing balls, dishing out feed, organizing games, and mediating in those pesky rawhide squabbles. It's tough being pack leader.

Yes, I said six. Two big, four little. I don't know how it happened.

Well first, I was worried about Sally. She's a little papillon, Doc is a big Lab mix. They weren't playing. Doc played with other dogs when we went to the park, but Sally just pasted herself to my ankles in her snooty way.

"Sally's very lonely," I said to everyone. "She needs a companion."

"Boy are you ever projecting," everyone said back.

I paid no attention and got Mike, a little papillon who was stranded in a kennel for months because he's half an inch too big to be a show dog.

Mike is the anti-Sally, fearful and nervous and prone to going for ankles. Only the toys that other dogs are playing with interest him. But he's pathologically affectionate and Sally loves him.

Then there's Homer, now lord of the couch, supreme raider of all wastebaskets.

The phone just rang. My editor wants my column.

"Listen," I yelled at her. "They all vomited this morning! All of them! Before breakfast!" She laughed. Laughed. Like it's funny. *Editor's note: I think it is funny.*

So then a woman at the park tried to give me Digby, this tiny scrap of a terrier. "We're Persian, we don't know how to care for dogs," she said. She was going to take him to the pound, so he's here being too goddamned endearing while I try to find him a home.

"Can't we keep him?" I constantly ask my son.

"We have too many dogs," he yells from his fortress of a bedroom.

The mailman just came. These dogs are such a cliché. But it's their only job, protecting the house. Every day they successfully rout the mailman and are thrilled with themselves.

Then there's Posy, a new arrival, a rescued papillon who had been used as a football—very abused, very nervous. In fact, she single-handedly started this morning's vomiting festival.

I sleep with dogs festooned on me. I eat with dogs crowded

around in an eager semicircle. Five of them accompany me on each and every trip to the bathroom (Homer won't abandon his couch), just in case I might need something. I am a frazzle.

I know what they're doing. They're trying to pull me over to the canine side. They are impatient with my foolish human conceits—wearing clothes, reading magazines, writing columns. They want me to scratch and sleep and run in circles and roll in smelly things.

Scary thing is, I'm beginning to see their point.

Editor's note: The last time she answered the phone, she barked.

Dear Problem Lady:

I thought that a person's unconscious mind was supposed to be a repository for all the secrets of the universe, that our actual consciousness was only the tip of the iceberg, and that all our real knowledge and deep connections with the Earth and everything really mythical about us were bubbling away under the surface and we could only rub shoulders with this majestic force within ourselves through dreams and such.

Imagine my surprise when I discovered that my own unconscious is a total moron.

The other day I found a half-starved little kitten on my fire escape and figured okay, fine, a kitten, and I took her in and fed her and named her Lucy, a nice name for such a cute scrap.

That night I had a dream. In this dream I realized the perfect, magical, incredibly apt and wonderful name for the kitten. Much better than Lucy. I woke up at 4 A.M. and savored the name on my lips.

"Noodle," I murmured and fell back to sleep.

The next morning I woke up and thought, "Noodle?" Then I lay there for a while, trying to figure out the name's deep resonance. There is none.

Noodle is a stupid, cutesy name. Someone who would name her cat Noodle is a person who would wear a "Kiss the Cook" barbecue apron and tape inspirational sayings on her refrigerator.

This is not the only thing that's happened. I've also concocted brilliant business strategies in my sleep, only to wake up and realize that many a fifth grader has done better.

So I live in a loft in Tribeca but my unconscious lives in a trailer park.

How can this be?

Sally

Dear Sally:

There are two kinds of unconscious thought. The kind you have in the shower, and the kind that tries to be clever when you're sleeping.

When you're in the shower, your unconscious is a witty, problem-solving, delightfully playful guardian angel. You shampoo your hair and the next thing you know an advertising campaign that will make you one billion dollars has sprung into your brain. You compose entire sonatas. You figure out how to ruin your exboyfriend's life without him knowing it was you. When you're in the shower, the force is with you.

Then there's the dark force. The brute unconsciousness with no intelligence or flair. This is the force that makes you go after men just like your father, abusive men who will go on three-day drinking binges and sleep with other women. The force that decides you don't deserve that wonderful job offer and gives you flop sweat and makes you gibber. The force that thinks having dreams about bananas and trains going through tunnels and naming your cat Noodle is all perfectly in order.

Our shower unconscious is our collective unconscious, it's the energy that binds us together and makes hundreds of writers suddenly think it's a great idea to write a biography of Hunter Thompson and thousands of women suddenly throw away all their miniskirts.

Whereas the dream unconscious is personal, full of symbolism about your rotten childhood and going to school without any clothes on to take a test you haven't studied for. You know, the stuff that's only interesting to you and your shrink.

Problem Lady

Dear Problem Lady:

Years ago, I named my dog Newt. Now what do I do?

Anti-Newt

Dear Anti:

Change his name to Snoot or Boot. He'll never know.

Problem Lady

Rush Limbaugh: Blow Me

Spay and Neuter Your Humans

*C*an we get one thing straight here? Do we or do we not believe in a collective unconscious? Is it true that we humans are not quite the isolated souls we sometimes feel like when we wake up too early on Sunday morning with nowhere to go and nothing to do? Is no man an island or what?

I say yes. I contend we shape each other's thoughts. Did one guy decide that all teenaged boys must, in 1994, wear clothes four sizes too big? No, it just pinballed around everyone's brain pans, it was everybody's idea all at once.

This is no idle speculation. This is serious. Just read the October 16 *New York Times Book Review* (it's in that pile shoved under your night table) and you will see that we are yet again at another crisis of humanity caused by bossy white science guys who don't believe in the collective unconscious.

White science guys are all very well, and sometimes even dreamy, but aren't they awfully linear? Don't they use statistics as weapons, the way white religious nut guys use the Bible to prove any cockamamie point that makes them rich? Don't white science guys filter their statistics and any other random factoid through their own muddled cultural prejudices and come up with gibberish?

The king of this kind of thinking is a "social scientist" named Charles Murray, a massively conservative guy who believes we should abolish all welfare, who once when a teenager burned ,a cross, who has now published a book with another guy about, among other things, how blacks are stupider than whites. The guy used the most exacting rigorous objective scientific experiments to rationalize his teen years.

Murray is one of the science guys who have taken on evolution, specifically how the human has evolved over millions of years with certain inalienable traits that guarantee his best chances of reproducing his own particular genes. It's the New Big Thing.

Didn't we see this coming? What with our obsessions about the ozone layer and the rain forests, with our newfound consciousness about animal rights, our fears that all the frogs were dying, didn't our little brains start noticing the interdependence among all life forms, thinking about trees and such, wondering where the hell we got the idea that humans were the be-all and end-all of the evolutionary trail with the moral right to spray deodorant up rabbits' noses? Didn't we start to wonder if the whole human species was this gigantic mistake?

The mass unconscious whirred away, cogitating on evolution, coming to its own intuitive conclusions, which in many cases had to do with humility, fear and recycling. Maybe, surely too late, we were frantically figuring out how to be proper humans in the world.

But then the bossy science guys, who are threatened by the very idea of a collective unconscious, galloped in waving and shrieking and telling us to stop thinking, to let a professional do it!

Out of the ether came many bossy white science books telling us what to think. Their version of reality, where everything is fixed and rigid, full of pointless detail and specious cause and effect, is utterly antiquated. They think we need traditional family values! That's their big answer!

Although their secret big answer is not to let those of the black "race"—like anybody's pure—have children. Because those of the black "race" score poorly on the white science guys' intelligence tests, okay? Because of all those out-of-wedlock children, right? Not because of prejudice or inner-city fear or anything, believe us!

"Sociobiology, hah!" says Dr. Michael Bywater, British authority on same. "You're applying an analytical tool to something that is only about 5 percent susceptible."

Even pure science is not pure of human taint. "The human observer constitutes the initial link in the chain of observational processes," says not-bossy physicist Fritjof Capra, "and the properties of any atomic object can be understood only in terms of the object's interaction with the observer. In atomic physics, we can never speak about nature without, at the same time, speaking of ourselves."

"Consciousness destroys the act," said William Blake.

The Darth Vaders of the force, white bossy evolutionists have disingenuously spewed out a noxious backlash of racism. Their "findings" will give overt and closet rednecks a glorious rationalization for their unspeakable thoughts and acts. And give those with racial guilt synthetic creepy cold comfort.

"They don't want to come right out and say it," says Michael Bywater, "but race is the only subtext. Life is an author that only knows one word . . . 'maybe.' Evolution is an editor that only knows one word, 'no.' That editor has one tool, and that tool is death. There is a negative selective pressure on American blacks. In three hundred years, unless things drastically change, there won't be any American blacks left."

And thus we continue on our merry way of that great American pastime, punishing the victim. No longer politically correct to say, but true anyway.

Polarity: A Lifestyle

*R*ight after the '94 elections you probably asked yourself, "Would it be so bad to be a Republican? Maybe they're all pro-life bigoted fascist assholes, but is that so terrible? Mario Cuomo's gone, Ann Richards's gone, I can either kill myself or go for a fitting at Brooks Brothers."

I would humbly like to suggest, yes, it is so bad. Just because we have recently had the trauma of watching George W. Bush smugly telling us that he is a "humbled soul," and then seconds later seen a shaken shrunken Cuomo quoting T. H. White, doesn't mean we have to throw in our personalities. The Republicans won but they are still big stupid lying bullies who want to make our wetlands into theme parks and get women back into their aprons and don't anybody fucking forget it for even a minute, okay? Okay.

This country, our beloved nightmare, has become completely polarized. It's them and us. Mantovani vs. Nine Inch Nails. And I have a proposal to make it easier for us, which we deserve since we're going to have to spend entirely too much time looking at Newt Gingrich. Let's escalate the polarity, make sure the entire fabric of society reflects our differences. Let's be Crips vs. Bloods. Well, maybe not. How's this: Furs vs. Flannels.

We Flannels must stand up for our rights! We must make our presence known! We must tailor our world so that we are not round pegs trying to fit into square fur life!

The first thing we change: Airline travel. Your typical flannel is most vulnerable when having to fly somewhere. Like, say he's a drag queen who has to change planes at O'Hare. Do you know what it does to expose your average drag queen to hordes of women in pastel stretch pants and gaily sequined sweatshirts, stampedes of men in ill-fitting blazers and tasseled shoes, or any sort of child whatsoever?

It makes your drag queen despondent, that's what it does, it reminds him of the miserable life he once had in Kansas City where nobody understood and everyone laughed at him.

What he and the rest of us artists and writers and poets and trendies and musicians and lounge lizards and just generally disaffected cynics need is an airport lounge. Not a "first class" lounge, no tacky Naugahyde high-flyer clubs with fax machines and awful businessmen swilling martinis, attitudinous women in hairdos and Hermès. We don't know these people, we don't ever want to. We want a "flannel" lounge full of puppies and pinball machines and extra pairs of black socks and no bad crackers and cheesefood, but plenty of Mallomars and murder mysteries. No beige, no maroon.

And then when we get on the plane, we want somewhere to sit. They can have "coach," they can have "first," we will have "alternate."

In alternate no one will thank us for choosing United, or ask us to include them in our future travel plans. The safety video will feature a drooling man on the verge of a seizure instead of a serene Stepford blonde. The music stations will never feature Kenny Rogers, the movies will be unedited Jarmusch and Campion. The flight attendants will have runs in their tights and wear vintage bowling shirts. There will be a bowl of complimentary condoms in the bathroom. The magazines will be *Wired, I.D., Garbage.*

In first class they can have gourmet dining, one million forks and wines, in coach they'll have mystery meat called *boeuf bourguignon* or *coq au vin* (used, of course, interchangeably), in alternate we'll all get a big mound of fries, nature's perfect food.

We need all this, and more. We're screaming nerve-jangled maniacs in a have-a-nice-day country. I urge the airlines to try this. We can't always go to England on Virgin.

Here's what else we need:

BANKS: Why do they all have to be like the principal's office? Why do the male tellers have to look like overcooked linguine and the females like tea cozies? We need banks with a properly sullen attitude, no passive-aggressive perkiness.

CRUISES: Wouldn't we like to get on a boat and run around in the Caribbean? We would, but not if there's any chance of running into Kathie Lee and Regis. How about a lovely ironic cruise, with *Brady Bunch* reruns and sock hops?

SHOPPING MALLS: Wait, there is one already! It's in Orange County and it's called the Anti-Mall and they've got threadbare furniture and Urban Outfitters. A start, anyway.

CARS: We don't want no Diamantes! No Celebrities! No Aspires! No Altimas, Achievas, Acclaims! No Spirits, Sonatas, Sables! How about a Honda Cynic, a Ford Excess, a Jeep White Bread? And enough with the beiges and the metallic silvers. What about yellow, orange, lime rickey?

HOTELS: Enough with the quilted mock-chintz bedspreads, faux gold leaf, and hideous seascapes. And if there's going to be room service, can they stop with the Shrimp Surprise and have more chocolate-chip cookies and milkshakes? We are not always in New York, where we can stay at the Paramount.

STATES: There are some perfectly gorgeous states, like Colorado and Oregon, but we can't live there because of the rednecks who hate drag queens. No, we have to stay ghettoized in nasty treeless cities full of sirens and smells because that's the only place we can see movies we like and find a coffee shop open at 4 A.M. I say we take over the pretty states. The rednecks don't care, they hate trees anyway and would be just as happy in Nevada living on an ex–nuclear test site. We could have great bookstores, jazz clubs *and* mountains.

Maybe we should just secede from the country completely. They'll never miss us. We sure won't miss *them*.

I'm PC, You're a Dickhead

I'm in a dither about political correctness. I can't decide if I think it's absolutely fabulous or a weird kind of liberal neo-Nazism.

As your basic left-wing tree-hugger, I decided early on that being PC was good. I stuck with this through the whole anti-PC brouhaha. Every time I saw an attack against PC in the media I figured some Republican asshole was behind it. Usually I was right.

But in the past week there have been two disquieting incidents.

I was at this party eating those blue tortilla chips you have to eat at parties these days and talking to one of those documentary filmmakers who have to be at parties these days. This one had taken the narrative for a film to some PC expert to get PC "clearance." Whatever the hell that is.

"Did you know," the filmmaker pointed out to me, "that you cannot use the word *nippy?*"

"You mean as in, 'Bring a sweater, it's a little nippy outside'?" I asked.

"Yeah," he said. "It might be construed as a slur against the Japanese."

"Get the fuck outta here," I said.

"Also, you can't use the word *slave,* because that may imply that someone is willing to be a slave. You have to use *enslaved person.*"

"Run that by me again?" I asked. He did. Twice. I still don't get it.

Then later on in the week I was attacked on national TV for my lack of correctness. Me.

I was on the panel of a talk show hosted by Mo Gaffney, a most excellent and hilarious woman. The show's topic was "Straight Women, Gay Men: A Beautiful Blendship?" Yeah, I know.

I was supposed to be the comic relief to some rather earnest gay-men-straight-women duos. The first thing I did on the show was get in trouble with them while trying to make friends during a break. "Hey, nice socks," I said to one guy. "Oh, but of course they would be, you're gay."

The four panelists glared at me. I told them it was a joke. That made it worse.

"Don't you see that it's wrong to stereotype a person like that?" said the socks guy's partner, a blonde in pink.

Later on I enraged members of the audience.

One person in the crowd stood up and proclaimed, "I've noticed that women who are friends with gay men are intelligent, creative, straightforward and independent."

"Of course," I said, "straight men hate women like that."

A man in the audience shot into the air. "That's a gross generalization!" he snarled.

"It may be a generalization, but it's not gross," said my Mo.

So I think that this earnest, more-correct-than-thou attitude is sanctimonious crap.

But then I immediately think that political correctness is much needed in America today. I know this because I have just returned from Portland, Oregon. There are some creepy, bigoted, fundamentalist assholes up there. If it weren't for a particularly vociferous contingent of PC types fighting the good fight, the spotted owl would already be history and an antigay bill would have become law.

"I'm so confused. Tell me what to think about PC," I said to my friend Michael Musto, a gay activist and fellow *Village Voice* columnist.

"I like it when it reflects an authentic feeling of outrage against prejudice," he said. "Like back when it was 'fighting homophobia,' or 'fighting racism.' But once it was called political correctness, it started to feel oppressive. You're afraid to say anything at all because it's bound to offend someone. The coalition of Filipino lesbians who are allergic to perfume might come after you.

"I once got creamed at Yale. I was on this gay panel, and someone asked, 'Do you think Vice President Dan Quayle is gay?' I said, 'He's much too stupid to be gay.' First they all laughed, then they attacked me for being offensive to straight people."

"So now we're not allowed to offend straight white men?" I asked. "They have all the power. We have every right to puncture their bloated self-opinions with humor. And as Bette Midler says, 'Fuck 'em if they can't take a joke.' "

"That's part of PC, being humorless."

"On the other hand, no one dares to say anything antigay now. It's very hip to be gay."

"I know," he said. "Every celebrity from Sharon Stone to Sarah Jessica Parker is constantly saying, 'I'm a gay man stuck in a woman's body.' This is a big advance over blatant homophobia, but I wonder what these people are really like, why they weren't like this before. Take Roseanne Arnold and Marky Mark—when they get the least bit ticked off, another person emerges."

This is the problem. Political correctness will change people's language and may therefore change their thinking. But consider a previous bout of political correctness, also accused of having no sense of humor, called women's liberation. Men at that time were incessantly saying, "Oh, my God, we were so stupid to oppress you like that. You're totally right. We'll never do it again. Hurry up, have a career while we do the laundry!"

They were kidding, of course. They mouthed the right platitudes while deep inside the hatred and resentment festered away unabated.

Then men exploded, spewing forth rancid antifeminist propaganda. Thus was the great backlash born.

PC may be positive in some cases and inane in others, but when it's simply camouflaging hatred, I'm against it. I like my hatred right out there where I can see it.

If I Were a Black Man

People would be scared of me. I just might like that. Now I walk down the street all soft and white and dawdling in front of Barneys windows while the Barneys doorman smiles and beckons, cracking the door, inviting me into an air-conditioned wonderland of three-hundred-dollar pillows, three-thousand-dollar suits and a five-thousand-dollar piece of pottery you don't even know what the fuck it is.

What would it be like to instead be a hard-bodied male and gleaming dark and people stepping out of my way or across the street even, grabbing tight to their purses and their shopping bags from the Pottery Barn containing teapots shaped like cabbages? The Barneys doorman would nervously pretend I was invisible. Korean grocers would see me at the salad bar and hope their surveillance cameras were working.

Would it be a kick to inspire fear just by my very presence?

I could walk down the street and not even worry about being raped. Even at three in the morning. Women of every size and age would scurry like ants in my wake, even if I wore a nice suit and wingtips and carried an umbrella. Of course, I might get shot.

And it might be hard to get a cab.

Would I feel odd reading books where white men are simply men but black men are black men? Or in old books Negro men, in new books Afro-Americans or persons of color? Would I feel singled out and special?

Would I feel battered by white people's hatred and fear? Would their constant attitude that I am not only inferior but expendable, that I am stupid and violent, seep into my soul and destroy my opinion of myself? Would I become full of festering self-loathing and get depressed and crave Prozac or Valium or heroin?

Or would I simply get angry, let the anger fuel me to be bigger and better and faster and scary and cynical and separate from everyone? Would I be clever, closed off and seething with hatred and distrust?

I guess I'd be both. I feel both ways now, even in my present incarnation as an invisible white woman, presumed to be incompetent and dependent, someone to bring the coffee. Even in my present soft white incarnation, I often dawdle down the streets with self-loathing and violence in my heart, lucky that heroin makes me puke, often awash with Valium to assuage the rage.

Now. If I were a black man, I'd have one of those pesky penises. And all its accoutrements. Testosterone for one, a stringently demanding hormone: I must compete. I must conquer. I must protect my loved ones, my home, my food, my possessions.

Plus I'd be inoculated from birth with America's rigid definition of masculinity: Be Arnold Schwarzenegger. Free and wild, chanting *"Hasta la vista,* baby" and "I'll be back," wasting bad guys with nary a blink.

But I'd be thwarted and betrayed. Testosterone and Arnold, it turns out, are property of white guys. A black guy may not protect or defend or say *"Hasta la vista."* He's supposed to be the cute roly-poly cop who eats doughnuts while Bruce Willis saves a whole building. Emasculated. Preferably wearing an anchorman hairdo.

Purported big dick making it all the more crucial—mustn't threaten purported pencil-dicked white boys.

I don't know if I'd like being a black man all that much.

But hey, whoa, hold the phone, what if I became a famous black man? Like an idol? A hero?

Say I started out my life living in my grandmother's brothel, or, I don't know, in the projects in San Francisco. A place where white people never go. Poor neighborhoods become exponentially more isolated every day that passes. No supermarkets or movie theaters. No interaction with the outside. An "us" and "them" mentality. A place portrayed as teeming with welfare cheats and junkies, not humans, certainly not potential friends. A place where young boys kill their brothers, where they implode.

And so if suddenly, through careening fate, I became everyone's darling? Everyone's beloved? On TV every minute? What if even the most poisonous bigot made an exception for me? What if when I walked down the street I would see the fear, scurrying and clutching of purses, then suddenly the shock of recognition and then I was everybody's hero?

Then I'd have it made, right? I'd be vindicated, happy.

But wait a minute. I had a soft, dawdling, fleeting brush with semi-fame a few years ago. I went to bed. If anything, fame hurt me. I was led to expect I would suddenly be completely different. I was still me.

So how would it be, being a megastar, getting everything anybody is ever supposed to want, which is all meaningless, and superimposing that on an incredibly damaged and battered ego? I might talk about myself in the third person. I might set fire to myself. I might bash in a car with a baseball bat.

If I were a black man, I don't think I could cope. Although could I be Patrick Ewing for just one day?

Good Old Days: Fact or Fiction?

*H*ello, I am a member of Generation X.

Okay, I'm not. I am a card-carrying hippie. But I am sick beyond death of old hippies. They've gone all sour and self-righteous. They're a bunch of soft, snotty know-it-alls.

Have you heard them lately? Here's the refrain: "Clinton sucks, he's not left-wing enough. Cars suck, they're not as cool as they were in the fifties when a Chevy looked like a goddamned Chevy. Topsoil sucks, don't even talk to me about topsoil. Music sucks and no wonder Kurt Cobain killed himself, his music was derivative crap. Radio sucks, I remember when the deejays could play what they wanted, now it's prepackaged, market-researched puke. Television sucks, I only watch PBS. Mention movies to me and I swear I'll have a grand mal, except for films from Nepal. These new little feminists suck, they don't know the *hell* we went through in the old days."

I say the old days suck. Because they're gone.

And no matter how cool and groovy and happening hippies were in 1966, that was like thirty years ago. Way past time to get over it.

And this saintly attitude? What are hippies anyway but failures? Lots of great ideas, great music, great drugs and tasty revolutionary rhetoric. Yeah, we were going to take over the world all right. With our be-ins and faces painted with flowers, we were going to show everyone that war was just plain wrong, and that we should all love each other indiscriminately and while we're at it, fuck each other indiscriminately. But first, pass me a tab of acid, okay? And what happened to the rest of that chocolate cake, man?

For every acidhead freak who is now a happy entrepreneur in Marin County, there is another acid casualty who is his janitor. For every righteous hippie with enough moral fiber to turn her back on capitalist culture, to stick to her back-to-the-land Commie ways, there are one thousand mired in the conundrums of whether they'll ever be able to afford a Jaguar and do they really have to stop wearing fur?

The hippies lost, okay? There was no revolution here. In other countries, yeah, and wasn't that fabulous.

My contemporaries are turning into my grandparents. Bitter antiques comfily and pointlessly ensconced in disapproval of the younger generation. Old farts who are no longer out there in the world, telling everybody else they're doing it wrong. I mean, please.

And could all old feminists whining about the younger generation please shut the fuck up? They're beginning to sound like stereotypical Jewish mothers. I have actually with my own ears heard a fifty-year-old feminist tell a thirty-year-old feminist, "You have no idea what I went through for you, don't you think you could show a little gratitude?"

Gratitude? The old feminists had all the fun. They worked within a cozy cocoon of sisterhood, warmed by the pungent mountains of burning bras, supported by legions of mea culpa male cheerleaders.

Now feminism is nuts and bolts, metallic and cold, undermined by male indifference and hostility. The thrill is gone, there's too much work to do. I kiss young feminists right on the mouth for persevering. I give them my firstborn son (actually, they've already got him).

Yes, the old days were better. Anything before AIDS was better. There are five times as many people in the world now as there were in 1850, and not a Dickens among us. Things were better before the industrial revolution, before the black plague, before the Inquisition and Christianity. Come to think of it, things were better before agriculture, back when humans were hunter-gatherers, when the unwieldy bodies we have now made perfect sense.

That's probably why the old hippies are whining so much. In the old days, in the really old days when the average human life span was thirty-five years, they'd all be dead. This will make your old hippie disconsolate.

Actually the world was better before humans altogether. No endangered species then. No ozone problems, plenty of frogs.

So we have two choices. We can take Generation X to our bosoms. I think apathy, depression, irony and confusion are damned fine ways to view a world going to hell.

Or we can really go back to the good old days. On the count of three, everybody shoot themselves.

Dear Problem Lady:

It was over in a blink of an eye.

I have long been this gung ho Bill Clinton person. I mean, really gung ho to the point where I did weeks of volunteer work—I even went door-to-door and called people up on election day. When Clinton won, it was like all the tension my body has been under for the past decade suddenly relaxed and I cried for half an hour with relief.

Even when I saw him waffling on Haitian refugees and gays in the military and taxing the rich I was fine. Transitions are rocky, people were pressuring him, it would all be okay.

When I saw Diane Sawyer interview Clinton on TV and he said protocol dictated that only members of his family and heads of state get to call him by his first name, and he figured it would be best to go along with the protocol, and when Hillary told Sawyer that she thought it would be "fun" to be called the "First Lady," I felt a small frisson. Why does such a guy of the people want to be called "Mr. President," and why does an alleged feminist ever in her life want to be called a "lady"? But I ignored my frisson.

Then last night I saw the inaugural ceremonies on TV. Barbra Streisand sang. She thought she was quite fabulous; her facial expression of smug self-adulation struck nausea in my soul. Let's face it, the funny girl's lost it, and who can blame her since she's incessantly surrounded by mewling sycophants constantly telling her she's the bee's knees.

During her songs the camera cut to Bill and Hillary, and Hillary was smiling that glazed smile she does for all public occasions, but Bill!

Bill had decided that he was in heaven! He was snapping his fingers and bobbing his head from side to side and acting as if he were about to have an orgasm, the music carried him away so much. You'd think he was listening to the Beatles reunited instead of Barbra look-at-my-legs-check-out-my-cleavage-and-did-you-happen-to-notice-my-nails Streisand.

It was so patently absurd, so clearly contrived, so lacking in dignity or judgment that all my hopes, all my lofty expectations, just shriveled and died on the spot.

The guy is just as dishonest and full of shit as everyone else! Nothing is going to change! Tell me the truth, is it time to emigrate to Canada?

Rachel

Dear Rachel:

Don't bother to emigrate, you are already on some galaxy far, far away. Bill Clinton is a politician. Politicians are required to be full of shit because they have to thread their ways to the top through the hordes of ambitious, narcissistic, amoral back-stabbing dickheads who run things in Washington.

This is not *Mr. Smith Goes to Washington,* Toto. Bill Clinton may be scum, but so far he seems to be our scum, who at least pretends to share the belief system of pinko-liberal-intellectual-gay-pride-espousing-Washington-marching-pro-choice-feminist-sympathizers like you and me.

We've got to let him act like an asshole sometimes. Let's just wait and see what he accomplishes.

Problem Lady

Dear Problem Lady:

I don't know how it happened. A month ago I was scrounging for spots in comedy clubs in Brooklyn, never even mind Manhattan, lucky if I had seven nasty coldhearted ex-felon drunks in the audience, then going home to my apartment on Avenue C with the bathtub in the kitchen, the toilet down the hall, and the extended family of mice under the coffee table.

And now I am the biggest thing in Hollywood. It all started with Judy.

Judy, twenty-five, blond, five feet tall, with her Chanel bag, Chanel earrings, Chanel shoes, Chanel bicycle shorts, and interlocking *C*s festooned on every part of her body, is a television network person. Somebody told somebody who told somebody else to tell Judy to see me, and there she was at 1 A.M. at the Gooforama Club where I'm fending off a puking guy with my microphone.

"Here's my card," says Judy, "call me in the morning."

So I did and next thing I know I'm flying to Los Angeles first-class surrounded by more blond women in even more Chanel playing with their Gameboys and adjusting their face-lifts and then I get to L.A. and sit in an office where several people in suits tell me I'm the next big thing and how would I like a truckload of money dumped right into my backyard?

Of course I say yes, although first I have to get a backyard. Which doesn't faze them in the least, they dismiss me with the wave of airy hands and say, "Out here we *all* have yards."

Which isn't true, is it?

Anyway, they all say, Don't worry we'll take care of everything, we'll find you a showrunner, he'll come up with an idea and you'll have your very own TV show and you are one lucky young woman, whatta talent, get yourself an agent.

So then, this is gut instinct, I hire the first agent who isn't wearing an Armani jacket, who turns out to be pretty nice and slightly sweaty and he says I get to say which showrunner I want.

So here are my questions. Will I have a yard? Will I sicken and eventually die in L.A., or is it not as bad as people say it is? What is a showrunner?

Valerie

Dear Valerie:

Congratulations. You are about to enter a game called "Hellfire and Damnation." The object of the game is to get one skillion dollars, and stay alive. The chances are maybe three thousand to one against you.

Just remember these handy rules:

1. You will probably lose. This is nothing to be ashamed of. F. Scott Fitzgerald and Dorothy Parker lost big-time. It is a badge of honor to be humbled, destroyed and driven insane by Hollywood, as long as you remember to leave.

2. Everything will be your fault. Yes, you are the hottest thing in the world right now, but everyone, except your network person, whose entire job and livelihood are dependent on your success, is dying for you to fail. If you choose the wrong showrunner who creates a lousy show for you, it's your fault. If the networks pit you against *E.R.* or *Seinfeld* and nobody watches you, it's your fault. If you call your show *PMS* and the members of PMS Anonymous, who think their problems are very serious and nothing to make fun of, decide to march around the studio chanting "PMS Kills!" thus frightening the networkers into quickly pulling your show off the air, it's your fault.

None of this would be your fault in the real world, but this is Hollywood, and you will acquire a bad odor. Everyone who said you were just the most genius will now be saying you are a lightweight, a flash in the pan, an embarrassment, a waste of space. So you have to get it right the first time or forget it.

3. Never, under any circumstances, listen to what the network persons tell you.

They know absolutely nothing, these networkers. They are business people. They will never go out on even a vague sort of a limb. It is possible that they would have the courage of their convictions if they knew what their convictions were.

Here are some shows utterly despised by their own network people: *Hill Street Blues. Letterman. Northern Exposure. Seinfeld. E.R.*

When a show, against all odds, turns out to be a hit, all network people have one simultaneous idea: "Let's copy it!" You go to meetings and they actually say, "Give us an edgy *Murphy Brown* with a touch of *Home Improvement.*"

Never in the history of television has a copy of a hit show ever been a hit. You can tell networkers this until you turn puce and expire. They won't believe you. And if you try to tell them they have to do something original, something creative, that even people in Peoria have brains, they call security.

So do what you want and tell them you're doing *Roseanne.*

Okay. A showrunner is someone who has already had a show on the air, someone of whom the networks approve. Being a career soldier, he (invariably he) will sell you out in half a second. He is a necessary evil. Get one who is only mildly paranoic-schizophrenic and who is very lazy.

You can have a backyard. You can even have a pool if you're a fool. But if I were you, I'd save every penny they give you, because here's the final rule: Always be ready to escape. Keep a suitcase packed.

Problem Lady

Pop Goes the Culture

Nice Girls Don't Read Romances

Permit me to introduce myself. My name has inexplicably become Cassandra.

My thick black eyelashes frame eyes the color of the skies in springtime. My complexion is creamy white with flushed cheeks, rosy lips, small white perfect teeth. My tiny waist can fit within a circle made by large, rugged, manly hands. I have glorious raven-black hair which I wear piled on top of my head, vagrant tendrils framing my lovely face. My breasts are high, large and handsome. My legs are long, my feet dainty. Also, did I happen to mention that I am a nineteen-year-old virgin?

Okay, I'm having a little trouble with the nineteen-year-old virgin stuff, but what the hell, I'll go with it for one very important reason:

Men want me. Bad. Short and tall men, ancient lascivious toads and pimpled squeaking youths all stutter to stunned silence when I waft into a room. Rich guys and royalty lay their hearts and plenty of diamonds at my beautifully shod feet.

Me? Diamonds? Royalty and rich guys? Cool.

Yes, I have been reading romance novels. Identifying with the heroines. It's a tough job, but someone has to do it.

I used to think that only, well, *trashy* women read romances. I see them all the time in airports and subways. They're always wearing housedresses or polyester pantsuits, or, if they're really fat, tight white leggings and an undersized T-shirt, and they're reading these books with their torrid, florid, unbelievably ugly covers full of Barbie dolls getting their dresses ripped apart by savage Ken dolls. These women always have slack jaws and glazed eyes and look like they're bingeing on mental Oreos. Sometimes they drool.

Whereas suited-up women or trendy green-haired girls are always reading Plato or something. Over the years I questioned various women I knew and they all denied any familiarity whatsoever with romance novels. Tacky and stupid, they said. Nice girls don't read romances, they said.

Turns out I am a dope. All the bookstores in my neighborhood have bigger and bigger romance sections, so I finally bought one. Jesus. They're masturbation books! Mostly "historical" stories, they are teeming with the hottest sex that can be described using incredibly clichéd euphemisms. Like this passage from a novel by Sandra Brown, current darling of the booksellers:

"Emboldened by his impassioned plea, she stroked and caressed until she found the smooth spearhead lubricated with the precious nectar of his desire. . . . His fingers found her feminine threshold moist and pliant and trembling. She tightened around his fingers like warm closing petals as they entered that haven."

And then they do it! After tons of sucking on her nipples in worshipful frenzy, he delves into her and fills her completely and they meet on this entirely new plane of awareness!

This book was really stupid and I hated it. I was utterly cold and blasé.

Okay, I'm lying. Every sex scene was built up so slowly, with excruciating attention to detail—how exactly the nipples were sucked and caressed, the texture of the skin, a plateau-by-plateau description of the orgasms, the rhythms of the thrusts—that I got into it. Just a little.

I decided to tell all the women I knew. They knew already. They just wouldn't admit it until I did.

"Oh, yeah, they're definitely a turn-on, although you feel kind of icky and stupid afterwards," said Rita.

"What are you going to do when you run out of fantasies?" asked Cleo, "go to the video store?"

Of course you're not. Even if you're not afraid of video store clerks giving you the hairy eyeball, porno videos cater to men's fantasies. The porno movies made for women are beyond dull, they never get it right. The closest thing to female pornography is *A Room with a View,* that Merchant-Ivory period drama where our hero is so besotted with our heroine, we think he may die without her.

Studying these conflicting fantasies, it's easy to understand why men and women have a tough time getting along well enough to get laid.

Women's romance pornography (Yes, that's what it is!) is incredibly involved with nice houses and costumes. The man must have valor, passion, social standing, rock-hard morality. And he must be so unbelievably obsessed with her that he's almost insane. Just the touch of the tip of her tiny finger throws him into uncontrollable frenzies. But he is honorable, and suffers his lust stoically. He has a great body. He wears really cool clothes. He really wants to take her out dancing and stuff. He really adores going down on her, and can always make her come.

"Yep, that about covers it," says Cleo, "although to me social standing means anybody who can play blues guitar."

In men's pornography the woman must be young and preferably naked. She must have incredible tits, and she must be begging for it. She loves to blow him, and really wants to bring another girl or two or even three along for the ride. She doesn't care for a second if she never sees him again, doesn't care about fancy restaurants or jewelry or anything but his big hard cock. And she always thinks he's big.

I think it's a good idea if we know about each other's fantasies. And if we let each other have them without whining. As long as we don't expect those fantasies to come true.

Compared to men's fantasies, I am one of those women on the subways I've been sneering at.

I won't be sneering at them anymore. Now I understand. Those women don't give a damn what they look like to me. They're immersed in a world where they are tender young maidens with raven-black hair and beautiful shoes.

The Celestine Cliff Notes

*O*ut in my garden the sun is shining, the flowers are preening, a bunch of blue jays are gangsta rapping. And I'm sitting here yearning for all of you in Manhattan, all smoking and drinking and shopping and cursing, all totally unaware of the spiritual revolution taking place west of the Hudson.

It seems there is this book, a "novel" called *The Celestine Prophecy*. I think it was published by a minuscule publisher in maybe Iowa or somewhere, then within a matter of seconds Warner Books snapped it up and it became the hottest thing ever and is perched atop the best-seller lists because it shows people The Way.

My friend Patti, her eyes aglow, pressed the book into my hands. Yesterday I started to read it. I turned the pages at an ever-quickening pace, devouring Patti's conveniently highlighted passages, my mind probing, spinning, marveling. At 2 A.M. I put the book down and swooned.

And here are my major words of wisdom for you: Avoid this book with every fiber of your being. It is mysticism for the mindless. It is cardboard writing for the reading impaired. It is Geraldo to Bill Moyers, *Barney* to *Sesame Street, The Bridges of Madison County* to *Lolita.*

But if you leave the tristate area for Memorial Day weekend you will inevitably find yourself amidst a horde of Celestomaniacs. You don't want to be caught short. You'll want to scoff convincingly. So here's the gist:

The Celestine Prophecy

Some nameless guy is restless and confused, even though he lives in splendor by his own lake. A friend appears from nowhere and says, "Go to Peru, there is a secret manuscript with nine insights."

The guy learns the first insight pretty quick: Humans are restless, they don't know why. They have been noticing increasing unexplained coincidences which are not coincidences at all but messages of mysterious coagulation of the Earth's forces.

The guy right away gets on a plane to Peru and is immediately beset by coincidences. Another guy waiting for the restroom is also searching for the manuscript and just happens to have the second insight: Humans used to believe absolutely in the church, but then they wanted more answers, the answers weren't quickly forthcoming, so they decided to start the industrial revolution and become greedy consumers.

When the guy gets to Peru everyone starts shooting at him because uptight priests are trying to suppress the sacred manuscript, but coincidentally a wise man intercepts him and takes him to a place of incredible beauty where he meets a sexy scientist and learns the third insight, which is full of quantum mechanics and unified field theory but boils down to the fact that we are all energy and if we stare at plants with love they will grow better.

But then more guys with guns come and the guy flees with the wise man and they keep meeting people whose cars have broken down who also happen to be searching for the manuscript. Then they go to a restaurant where a couple is yelling at their daughter and discover the fourth insight: People compete for energy, they will try to control one another to steal each other's energy.

Then more guys come with guns and our guy goes to a mountaintop where there's a virgin forest and he has a mystical experience where he feels connected to the whole universe and gets a huge injection of energy and this is the fifth insight.

Then our hero meets a priest who tells him he is too aloof, because his parents made him that way. People can either be aloof, interrogators, intimidators or poor-me types, depending on their childhood dramas or, if you will, scripts. Discovering your personal drama is the sixth insight.

Oh yeah, the sexy scientist is captured by guys with guns.

Then soldiers also capture the guy and take him to a nice clean prison where he keeps having fantasies about the sexy scientist and lo! there she is in a fetching prison outfit. A young prison inmate explains the seventh insight: Pay attention to all your day-and night dreams, they all turn out to be true. Nothing and nobody crosses your path by accident. If you keep running into the same person, this is destiny. Ignore it at your peril. (There was a guy named Howie Guttenplan. I would run into him anywhere I went in Manhattan, almost every day. Oh, Howie, what have we missed?)

The guy and the sexy scientist escape and learn the eighth insight, which is to give people good energy but not get addicted to any person, because that will cut off true energy. (Howie, maybe we had a lucky escape!) Our guy and the sexy scientist kiss and become addicted to each other and have to part.

Then at these ruins the guy meets all the people who had appeared during his journey and learns the ninth insight: Humans will decrease their population and evolve so that they will no longer need money, they will have incredible technology and everyone automatically will have everything they need. Plus they will let the forests grow back.

And then humans will vibrate at such high energy levels that they become invisible!!! That's what happened to the Mayans!!!

The End

Smart People in L.A.!

WARNING: This is not a column. This is a lame, half-baked, quarterhearted, self-indulgent excuse for a column. The "columnist" may not be held responsible for any excessive head-scratching, dozing or irate exclamations along the lines of "They *pay* her for this?" amongst her readership.

On Friday I lost my car. I needed to get studded biker cuffs and assorted chains and boots for the dominatrix/bondage look I was going for in my new incarnation as go-go dancer for the Rock Bottom Remainders, a rock and roll band full of authors who get to live their teenaged fantasies by playing gigs for book-oriented people who really try hard to believe they're listening to a real band.

Los Angeles was hosting the ABA, the yearly convention of publishers, bookstore owners, distributors, sales reps, authors' escorts, publicists and authors, all madly going to hundreds of parties in order to obscenely suck up to each other. It was a wondrous prospect for me stranded here in L.A., there would be humans using words other than "yeah," "uh," and "residuals." Somebody might even say "sonnet."

I was so excited and exhausted from bondage shopping that I

forgot on which side street off Melrose I parked my car, and wandered around panicking for forty minutes, finally finding my gigantic moving handbag full of hot Diet Cokes, dog leashes and forgotten dry cleaning. It was my third happiest moment of the weekend.

My second happiest moment I wasn't even there for but I heard about it. Some agent who used to be Swifty Lazar's sidekick gave a party with three guests of honor. The first honored guest droned on so long that the other guests got bored and began chatting. She spoke louder, they chattered louder until she huffed off. The second honored guest tried out his speech to complete indifference and louder chatting. Then the agent-host said, "And now, ladies and gentlemen, the moment you've all been waiting for, our main guest of honor, Kirk Douglas!!!"

Mr. Hollywood Royalty appeared, humble, ready for adulation. Nobody gave a shit. They just kept talking foreign rights and gossiping, not caring if Kirk lived or died. Kirk was stunned. He started sputtering, then screaming abuse at the crowd and finally just went insane with fury. It was too fabulous.

I did get to go to the authors' escort party, where all the authors' baby-sitters from all over the country vote on who was the past year's most obnoxious author and unveil that author's face on a dartboard. Jeffrey Archer is a favorite. This year everyone was torn between Tony Curtis (snapped orders at everyone, had temper tantrums, wife refused to speak), Betty Friedan (just generally behaved abominably) and some guy named Dean Ornish, who slammed a car trunk on an escort's head, causing profuse spurting of blood, then wondered petulantly how he would get to the airport.

This year the escorts' dartboard award went to . . . nobody. The wimps. Most of them wanted Betty fervently, but they thought she was too old and anyway it would be politically incorrect.

I went to a party at the Playboy mansion where nobody was allowed inside, but Hef wandered outside for a while. Clarissa Pinkola Estés, Ph.D., hypnotized me by the monkey grotto. I was a bit concerned because I had written possibly a tiny bit nastily about her book, but she showered me with love anyway. P. J. O'Rourke theorized it was the old mafia idea of "Keep your friends close, keep your enemies closer."

P.J. and I drove past L.A.'s hottest, trendiest, grooviest, most happening new nightclub, the House of Blues. It is a synthetic Texas roadhouse with synthetic graffiti. "Look," P.J. said, "faux dirt!"

Sane, cynical people in L.A.!

Then it was time for the sound check for the Remainders. The go-go dancers, guided by go-go mom Lorraine Battle, figured out some slapdash, haphazard choreography. We had actual *cages*. I, a feminist, was offended.

Then I went home and collapsed and noticed that my dogs, because of my continued absence, had had a collective temper tantrum and peed all over the house.

Then I went back to the Hollywood Palladium for our gig. Backstage, Amy Tan organized her whip and wigs, Stephen King moodily (shyly?) smoked cigarettes, Dave Barry cavorted with Kinky Friedman, Ken Follett borrowed his wife Barbara's eyeliner, Kathi Goldmark wriggled into a prom dress, Matt Groening and Roy Blount, Jr., were their beatific, adorable selves.

Visitors appeared. Erica Jong, now author of *Fear of Fifty*, wanted badly to go-go dance and almost decided to. Bruce Springsteen, friend of Remainder Dave Marsh, appeared with beard. Everyone went berserk. I thought, Oh, big deal.

Then the show started and I fell in love with my cage (so safe!) and gyrated my brains out and tossed my hair everywhere. The crowd roared for a bunch of not really too young or musically talented authors.

For the last number Bruce Springsteen came out to sing "Gloria." As I sang backup at a mike with Ken Follett, I suddenly realized what I was doing. Singing, onstage, with the Boss. Whoa. That was my favorite moment: Maybe in my life.

The World According to *AbFab*

*S*weetie sweetie darling sweetie darling sweetie. . . . One more face-lift and she'll have a beard, sweetie. . . . Stopped drinking, it was the worst eight hours of my life, darling. . . . Make Mummy coffee, darling, you're so clever, you know where everything is. . . . She's so anal, she sits on a sofa, sucks it right up. . . . Lacroix, sweetie, Lacroix!

Oh, hello. I was just in a reverie (darling). I was just sitting here, drinking Diet Coke and watching my cellulite multiply (sweetie) and laughing.

That's right, sweetie, laughing at cellulite! Which would never happen if I were doing normal, red-blooded, American masochistic things like reading *Vogue* magazine or watching network TV, but I am having my own personal *Absolutely Fabulous* festival. I don't have to watch it anymore, I have an internal tape loop running. It's the only sitcom for women with big attitude problems, for women who refuse to love too much.

Until now, I had to content myself with heros from the forties. Myrna. Roz. Not Thelma or Louise, they die, what good are they? Not Roseanne, her personal monstrosities have eclipsed her

TV persona. Not Kathie Lee or Katie or Barbara or any of those news babes who speak to the bikini-waxing, Club-Med-going, blow-dried, manicured marriage-minded.

Thank God for Edina and Patsy. Drinking like fish, evil and foul-tempered, hugely shallow, greedy and lustful, they make perfect role models. *AbFab* gives me a reason to live. I pretend I'm Patsy, give people pills, say "Don't question me!" When my kid dares defy me, I become Edina and threaten to adopt several Romanian babies. I plan to fall drunkenly out of taxis whenever possible. Patsy can't remember ever going to sleep, she passes out instead. I shall emulate her.

"We only get it on cable," I've been telling people since I arrived in England two weeks ago. "The big TV networks don't think Patsy and Edina are positive role models."

All I get are dazed and confused limey looks. *AbFab* is huge over here, even scabrous right-wing Tories and gardening grandmas piss themselves laughing at it. This proves that even though the English have taken to putting pineapple *and* lettuce on their pizzas, they are still the most civilized. They see no advantage or point to positive role models.

Neither did we, twenty or so years ago. I wonder if we realize how slowly but inexorably the world of normal, upstanding, silly people has crumbled, how America has been replaced by a Stepford country.

My clearest example of this phenomenon is the movie *M*A*S*H*. Do you remember? There was that constant loudspeaker in the background, with Radar or someone making announcements. One of the announcements was how a shitload of methamphetamine was missing. Just a little joke. Never mentioned again, not a plot point.

No, a plot point was Frank Burns getting down on his hands and knees, praying to God. That moment was there expressly to show the audience that Frank Burns was a bad guy. An uptight, weak, dishonest, self-aggrandizing, hypocritical, priggish dork.

I can't imagine a movie now where a character getting down on her knees and praying to God would mean she was unsavory.

I was driving on the wrong side of the road today, listening to BBC radio, and there was an interview with some athlete. The show was called something like *Soapbox,* the format was famous people giving alternative viewpoints.

This guy's alternative viewpoint was that he was a born-again Christian. He kept apologizing and trying to prove he wasn't weird or anything, saying that he knew people thought he was out of his mind but really, no kidding, he had written a book to prove that Christianity is absolutely fabulous. His listeners scoffed.

I was so exhilarated that I hardly noticed forcing a huge truck (lorry) into a tree and sideswiping a Land Rover. Here was an entire country of people who spoke a very similar language, yet none of them feared the fundamentalist right. They call them God-botherers.

In America the thought police have managed to have a stranglehold even on our subconscious. We're scared of them, we should be, because they shoot abortion doctors. But we also are resigned to them. We think it's normal to have fanatics decide what's on TV. We can't even conceive of a land where the inmates run the asylum, where uptight authority is slammed against the wall, where peace, love, hippies and decadence are normal and cherished. Where women can be mad and bad and not get punished.

I think Big Brother did appear in 1984, but by then we were so cowed we didn't notice. And we take it for granted that this monolithic Big Brother is watching us closely so we'd better be very, very careful to conform.

Only Patsy and Edina, our heroes, can lead us out of the mire. Sweetie.

Old Guys Amok
in Hollywood

I'm not bitter. I'm not angry. I think it's perfectly okay that I live in a town where it's normal for old guys of seventy to have teen-aged wives, a town where women are considered over the hill when they're twenty-eight, not to mention politically incorrect if not blond. I suppose I could be upset that in this town guys my very own age, with a similar frame of reference and political outlook to mine, wouldn't for a second consider dating me, that the oldest woman they deem appropriate is, say, thirty-three. It's true that this sucks in a big way, but I can always move to Oregon, and I just might.

But what does bother me just a teensy bit is that these old guys have conspired to subvert and corrupt the entire world with their sicko predilections.

In 1988, Sally Field played Tom Hanks's love interest in *Punchline*. In 1994, in *Forrest Gump*, she plays his mother. We'll have a moment of silence while I let that sink in. On my TV screen right now is a commercial for *I Love Trouble*, a love story starring Julia Roberts and Nick Nolte, a man who could, if pressed, be Julia's grandfather.

How crazy is this? How egomaniacal and hostile to the women and men of America (no, wait, the whole world!) who plunk down their six or seven dollars plus another fifty bucks for popcorn, etc., to sit in a darkened theater in order to get swept into a story that will either distract them from their miserable lives or maybe even give them new hope and insight into same lives? Why should they be subjected to unattractive and pointless fantasies? And what if they try to model their lives after such drivel? That shit does not play in either Peoria or Paris. Everybody loses, nobody gets laid.

The media, some say, rule our consciousness. Television and movies tell us what to think. Luckily this is not totally true. Luckily most of us have a few unclaimed brain cells, or we would simply accept as normal that although Jack Nicholson was once Shirley MacLaine's romantic lead, he is now in *Wolf* with decades younger Michelle Pfeiffer, who also gritted her teeth and tried to play the love interest to grandfatherly Sean Connery. And meanwhile Ann-Margret, whom Jack treated abysmally in *Carnal Knowledge,* is way too old to be considered sexy unless she's with Walter Matthau and Jack Lemmon, who had a big romance with Shirley MacLaine in *The Apartment,* but Shirley couldn't be in *Grumpy Old Men* with Walter and Jack because she was busy being a dying eighty-year-old in *Guarding Tess.*

Wasn't Faye Dunaway fabulous with Jack Nicholson in *Chinatown*? Now she would be deemed way too old. Now we have to watch him with babies two generations younger.

Just like his pal Warren Beatty, another man whom Faye Dunaway helped make famous. Warren in his time has also starred with Natalie Wood, Vivien Leigh, Eva Marie Saint, Jean Seberg, Leslie Caron, Susannah York and Paula Prentiss (all gone) and Goldie Hawn (trying hard not to be gone). You will no longer see him anywhere near his erstwhile leading ladies Diane Keaton and Julie Christie. He is over Madonna. Annette Bening is what, twenty-seven?

I miss Julie Christie mightily. Diane Keaton got to play the lead with Woody Allen, who in real life is with Soon-Yi. But would Diane ever be cast with Al Pacino, with whom she had a long on- and off-screen romance? Now it is allegedly appropriate that Al star with Penelope Ann Miller, who I think is twelve.

"I call her Cantaloupe Ann Miller," said Teri Garr, giggling. "No reason. I just like to."

I am delighted that Teri Garr is my friend, since I worshipped at her feet in *Tootsie,* etc. There is a downside, however, to our friendship. "I wouldn't kick her out of bed," says Don, whom I crave in bed. "I've had a crush on her my whole life," says Mark, who recently informed me that he wants to be "just friends." "I want her so *bad.* I have to sleep with her," says my son's roommate.

But do the Hollywood old boys make us all happy and cast her as a leading lady?

"If I got a bunch of plastic surgery so that I looked thirty-two, I still wouldn't *be* thirty-two," said Teri. "The best I can hope for is to play a mature woman who's still feisty and interesting and maybe sexy. Lauren Bacall told me that Jennifer Jones said that after a certain age an actress should never leave the house. Is that supposed to be my fate? Gena Rowlands, the most beautiful and fabulous actress, said to me, 'Wait until you get a review that says you've been ravaged by time.' I guess that's like being ravaged by a fierce tiger. Only worse."

A couple of L.A. deejays, the day after the Academy Awards, were so nauseated by the sight of ex-babe Deborah Kerr, they decided they would never marry.

"Men in this town carp about women getting older as if they're doing it just to piss them off," said my friend Carlene. "At the magazine stand last week some guys were looking at a photo of Mary Tyler Moore and saying with horror, 'God, she's getting OLD!' It's okay for a guy like Johnny Carson to be old, but they act like women are playing this hideous trick on the world."

It's not like these old guy–young broad movies are commercial blockbusters. Nobody in the real world wants to see them. We'd much rather watch soaps, thank you, where Erica Kane still gets the pick of the litter. But Hollywood is powered by immensely neurotic guys who need to own seven Jaguars and live in an ornate fantasy world. I have seen, firsthand, way too many instances of their fear and loathing of older women.

"Guys out here have all run away from home, they've gotten as far away from their parents as possible," said Stuart, a movie producer. "They're all lousy with unresolved Oedipal problems."

Fine, but could they please stop taking it out on the rest of us? I miss Meryl Streep and Jessica Lange.

Dear Problem Lady:

I used to snort coke, I used to take quaaludes, I've been a eating binger, I've had a six-pints-of-beer-a-night and three-packs-of-cigarettes-a-day habit.

You could say I have an addictive personality and I wouldn't argue. I thought I'd cured myself. I had tons of therapy and went to myriad twelve-step programs and I was actually to the point where I'd never mention higher powers or use the phrase "one day at a time," and all my friends liked me again. But now something horrible has happened. A new addiction has got me by the throat.

Computer solitaire. You know, you boot up Windows, and you can go into your regular writing program or you can click the mouse onto "games" and lose yourself for an entire day putting red sevens on black eights and trying to score over five thousand.

I actually play until I feel sick to my stomach, like I've eaten too much sugar or something. But do I stop? Hah. It's always "just one more game," and next thing I know it's three in the morning and I've forgotten to have dinner.

I'm probably going to lose my job as a secretary, which is a horrible job anyway and who can blame me for playing solitaire instead of getting out one million bullshit business letters, but what about my career as a secret novelist? I had almost two-thirds of the book done before this misbegotten game reared its ugly head.

I guess I just want to fail. I guess psychologically I can't bring myself to finish my novel and let the world, or at least some agent, see it. But wouldn't you think after all the therapy in the world I'd be better adjusted?

Elaine

Dear Elaine:

It's not you, it's the game. It induces some kind of brain state halfway between transcendental meditation and a heroin rush. This game is about to bring the entire world's economy to a standstill, since everybody has it on their computers and nobody has the willpower anymore to wrangle with spreadsheets.

There is only one thing to be done. A desperate measure, but it just might work. Get rid of Windows. Just wipe it right out of your hard drive. In fact, get rid of your hard drive. Go back to the elementary word-processing programs that can fit on a floppy.

Otherwise you're screwed. The demon game will never let you go.

Problem Lady

Dear Problem Lady:

The magazines are showing resort wear, which means I've got to look at a bunch of almost-naked models and want to kill myself. I look at those sculpted upper arms, those thighs without a hint of cellulite, those flat stomachs, and I am so overcome by jealousy that I would pay half my annual salary to exchange bodies with Naomi Campbell.

Is there any way I could make this happen?

Tania

Dear Tania:

You could make a deal with the devil. But I wouldn't.

We are our bodies. No, really. The body and the mind are intertwined in more crucial ways than we have ever imagined.

These days your enterprising therapist will press on her patient's forehead or shoulder or something and the patient will suddenly erupt with heretofore blocked childhood memories, burst into tears, and then feel a whole lot better. Actual memories are held in our muscles. Goofy, but true. Ever start sobbing in the midst of, or after a massage? Now you know why.

Which means that if you exchanged bodies with a model and then went to one of these newfangled shrinks, she'd press on your neck and you'd suddenly remember some junior high lip-gloss fiasco that never happened to you at all.

You'd probably have a different personality altogether. You'd start liking Michael Bolton. Death is better.

Take your body under your wing.

Problem Lady

Dear Problem Lady:

Do I have to wear Dr. Martens with flowered dresses?

I know you're supposed to. Well, not that you're supposed to, but everyone does. No, that's not right either. If you want to look cool and happening you do.

I've always craved flowered dresses but I've always been afraid I'd look too Laura Ashley, so I hid my perverse desires. I'd buy the dresses and then hide them in the closet.

But now they've come out. And I'm thrilled except when my friends look sarcastically at my delicate sandals and wonder why I'm not wearing combat boots like everyone else. Well, not everyone, but you know.

Anyway, what about penny loafers?

Cecile

Dear Cecile:

I suppose if your friends told you to jump right off the Empire State Building and into a Liz Claiborne shirtwaist, you'd do that too.

Problem Lady

Sisterhood Is Everywhere

Guns and Poses

*Y*esterday I attended a workshop in Phoenix called "Women's Empowerment in the Nineties." You're picturing a bunch of broads sitting in a circle, whimpering about low self-esteem and how to find the right mate, right?

Wrong. Get out of the eighties, suckers.

Okay, we did sit in a circle until the guns came out. We even shared our feelings.

"There's a man stalking me," said a horse breeder.

"My friend was murdered last year," said an insurance underwriter.

"I've been robbed, beaten up, raped," said a union steward. "I have an automatic and a .38 special. I don't want to be a victim anymore."

"I'm here because my husband says you're absolutely marvelous," said a medical technician.

"Thank you, I like to hear that from a man," said Paxton Quigley, our workshop leader. An odd thing to say, I thought. But everything struck me as odd. I was in a place called Shooter's World, which I can't even begin to describe except to say it's a huge place brimming with weapons and weapon accessories. Plus a gun range and a couple of conference rooms. Normally you won't find me in such a place. I wouldn't have thought you'd find Paxton Quigley either—with her Beverly Hills–coifed blond hair and fancy python boots, she looks like every woman in a BMW. But here she was, wispy and little, teaching twenty-six young to middle-aged women how to kill—no, sorry—*stop* their attackers.

Before we got to the hard stuff, we learned how not to be stalked. We learned to never have addresses on our checks, to always lie when merchants ask for phone numbers, to use mean and threatening as opposed to submissive eye contact, to always watch a man's hands, to barricade ourselves in our bedrooms and bathrooms behind a solid-core door with a Medeco lock and maybe even an aluminum sliding door, to ram a car in precisely the right place when it's trying to force us off the road, to spray an attacker's face with red pepper spray which will disable him for thirty minutes.

"I'd like to talk briefly about oral sex," Paxton said. "You *can* bite it off. I hope you never have to, but you do have the power to do that."

Then we had lunch. Turkey and ham sandwiches. I made friends with Laura, who writes sci-fi books; Gladys, an NRA instructor; Betty, a Burger King manager; and Pat, a gorgeous woman wearing a T-shirt that read "When only cops have guns, it's called a police state."

After cookies Paxton had us stand in a circle and chant, "Get the FUCK outta here!" in our meanest, most threatening voices. Paxton had interviewed rapists in prison and discovered they don't like dirty language from a victim. Laura had a hard time with this, she kept giggling submissively and blushing with the fear of expressing anger the way we women are taught.

Then it was gun time. I was agog as half the women in the room pulled guns from holsters in innocent-looking purses. The rest of us were given a revolver for a day.

"You want a .357 Magnum?" Paxton cooed.

"Sure," I cooed back. First we practiced with dummy bullets. We loaded, aimed, unloaded, learned how not to shoot ourselves in the foot.

"The head is the person," said Paxton. "I want you to get used to shooting to the head."

Then we put on protective headsets and glasses and walked to the gun range. "I don't know," said Pat, "a lot of ditzy women with loaded guns in one room."

"Come on, we finally have a teacher who's not calling us 'honey,' " said Betty.

I was fucking terrified as I stood, loaded gun in hand, in front of a paper target stenciled with a male silhouette. I was afraid I'd panic, and when I panic I get stupid. So I went slow. I aimed. I shot. I hit the target in the head and neck. I stared at the target, imagined blood running from the holes, felt sick.

"You blinded him, he can't see. You got him in the neck, he can't talk!" yelled a beautiful blonde.

We went through several exercises and several rounds of ammo. We shot slow, fast, one-handed, stationary and moving toward the target. We learned the Mozambique, one shot to the head, two to the chest. "That's my favorite," said Paxton.

"It's a rush, isn't it?" said Pat.

I was shooting cautiously when Gladys the NRA instructor came up. "Come on, get the son of a bitch," she said. I felt a surge of adrenaline and pulled off two perfect shots.

"Okay, I want you to build up some aggression," said Paxton. "Yell at the target as you shoot this time."

"That's for talking down to me!" yelled Betty.

"Go fuck yourself, you bastard!" yelled Pat.

Our last exercise was shooting at the targets through our wide-open knees while lying flat on our backs. From the about-to-be-raped position. I pulled off five perfect shots to the chest. I was getting good.

"How many women would just love to do this at the gynecologist's office?" Betty asked, and many hands shot up.

After two hours of shooting the workshop was over and we were bushed.

"This ass kicking sure takes a lot out of you," sighed Pat.

I said good-bye to my new pals and collapsed on a bench outside Shooter's World, feeling unsettled. I decided to dismiss the whole thing. These women were a bunch of Dirty Harriets who were attracted to violence. Who said they hoped they'd never use their guns but secretly wanted to. Right-wingers. Not like me.

Not like me. I've never been attacked, raped, beaten.

I stared into space for a few minutes. Then I walked back into Shooter's World and bought myself some red pepper spray.

Is Female Feminine?

I've been cooking. People are flabbergasted.

"You're just our own little Martha Stewart," says Lynn Ann.

"It's scary," says Cleo, "you're turning into a real *ballabusta*." This is a Yiddish word that means career housewife, and is obviously the root word for *ballbuster*.

They're teasing me and watching me squirm and deny my incredible chicken soup prowess, they know the last thing I want to do is *tip the balance*.

I've already got some feminine attributes. I am massively maternal, nurturing everything I see, watching with sheer fulfillment as my dogs inhale their kibble and broccoli, as my cacti grow flowers. Plus I am bad at sports, have big tits and bigger hair. And I've got lacy curtains. So I'm on the edge.

All I need now is to stop smoking and swearing. Maybe wear little heart earrings and a ribbon around my neck, know how to use Woolite. Wear fluffy embroidered sweaters. Use a pumice stone. Know the difference between cologne and toilet water (my dogs sure do). Get a bikini wax. Get a bikini.

I am going to be sick. Feminine means marginal, feminine means childish. Or that's what it feels like when I roll it around in my head.

But wait, what's wrong with being maternal, having big tits and lacy curtains?

Society belittles feminine things. Macramé and embroidery are foolish pastimes, drinking beer and watching football perfectly groovy. It's a big insult to be told you "throw like a girl." Women wearing men's clothes are *chic,* men wearing women's clothes make us fall on the floor laughing. Being an old woman means being fearful and wimpy. Being an old man just means being dirty.

Then there are the things that are designated feminine. Gossip. Cattiness. Spending all day in the bathroom getting your hair right. Obsessions with outfits. Excessive phone usage. Extreme sensitivity. These are not feminine traits, these are teenaged traits.

Still, being called feminine is something I do not desire. There is more to it than potpourri and ankle bracelets.

Being feminine means you always smell good, which means you never sweat which means you never exert yourself which means you never go after what you want. You must also smell good "down there" or else you'd better spray on some of that feminine hygiene deodorant which makes your vagina smell like your linen cupboard. It means being a lady, holding back, never laughing too loud or too long, never making off-color jokes, never really making jokes at all, but giggling demurely at all the jokes that men tell you. It means putting your hands on your hips and stamping your little high-heel-shod feet when you're annoyed, a picture of cute helplessness. It means telling men how big and strong they are and letting them have the remote control. It means letting the man hold the door for you and pay the check; maybe if you're good at it he'll throw his coat over rain puddles in your path. Never shouting like a "fishwife." Giggling and blushing at improper words or advances. Not being good at math or science and never ever knowing where the carburetor is, or even knowing how to change a tire or pump gas and, let's face it, driving like an idiot. Being feminine means being flustered easily, not being able to take pressure, it means holding your opinions back in conversation, always putting others first.

Submitting. Being helpless. Needing men to care for you. Never being pushy or aggressive.

Being feminine means existing only with men's sufferance. Do any men even want this anymore? Do any men need this kind of simpering behavior to bolster their egos? Please. Femininity is a dinosaur.

Femininity and being female are not interchangeable.

Last year at Thanksgiving I conducted an impromptu experiment. Everyone was sitting crammed into a smallish space, all of them in deep conversation. You couldn't get by anyone without them scrunching up their legs. As I wove through the crowd, I would always have to say "excuse me," sometimes twice, to the men. The women all saw me in their peripheral vision and would tuck their legs back smoothly without missing a beat in the conversation.

I don't know what this means. It's a nature vs. nurture thing. The nature folks would say it's something to do with women's right and left brains being more connected. The nurture people would say that women have had it hammered into both brains to look out for the needs of others.

But I do know that being female, no matter what age, sexual orientation or race, is full of such striking small details.

Being female means being intimate with blood. It means thinking that is more cyclical than linear: Believing in stars and such, watching flowers blossom and die and blossom again, being terrified that the blood has soaked through our jeans onto an upholstered armchair. It means insecurity: Does he like me? Does she like me? What does it mean when he says this? Why won't she say that? How can I look prettier? Why is my hair the only hair in the world that never looks good? Being female means defensiveness as a way of life: When wearing a skirt, keep your legs always together unless you are Sharon Stone making a movie. Do not invite virtual strangers into your home. Do not go out walking in the park or anywhere at night alone. Being female means being fiercely protective: Fuck with my husband, my children, my animals, my plants, my house or my new shoes and I will rip your head right off your body.

Being female means coping with this insane life, always taking into account the gorgeously absurd accessories God or evolution gave us.

Being female is a bitch.

Girls' Night Out: Why?

"Oh, God, my tits hurt so bad," said Kitty. She was dressed slickly chic but looked wan and frazzled. "Weaning a baby is the end of the world. I want to die." She put her head on my shoulder. "I feel like something scraped off the bottom of a shoe."

Jane, swathed in Armani, tsk-tsked smugly. She herself had just become pregnant and she was irradiated with her secret.

"Don't wean," I said to Kitty. "If it hurts that much it's too quick and too early. Leave it for a couple of months." Kitty's eyes filled with tears, maybe of joy.

"Easy for you to say, you only had one," said Sarah. "The second time you're ready to wean ten minutes after your milk comes in."

"Don't you hate it when the milk comes in so quickly that you suddenly have two *rocks* on your chest?" said Valerie, who had been silent until now.

We were at an official Girls' Night Out, and I couldn't figure out what I was doing here.

You too may have noticed the constant features in "women's pages" of newspapers about how there's the groovy new phenomenon, Girls' Night Out. How everybody who's anybody is eschewing men for one night a month, when they all get together and I guess let their hair down. How liberating and refreshing it is not to have stupid guys around belching and farting and talking football. How wonderful it is to *bond* with other females, to be able to speak out on any topic you want to without those judgmental, masculine scowls.

I find the whole notion profoundly depressing. It's so very ladies-protesting-too-much. The general tone and the women quoted in these articles sound so upbeat, perky and utterly desperate. "Oh, no," the women say, "we don't need men, we can be perfectly happy with just each other!" Which, decoded, means "Get me a boyfriend before I go out of my mind!" or, if you have one, "Lay a finger on my man and I'll break your leg!"

To make such a fuss of Girls' Night Out, to use words like "just each other," means there is an ugly subtext going on, a depraved presupposition that men are the superior sex. That women have to use all kinds of special props and pep talks to define themselves without men.

Not that I'd actually been to one or anything. I figured it would be just like when you see those women watching male strippers (that I've done *once,* okay?) and they clap and carry on and act the way that they think men act, the way men watching strippers in movies act. Actual men watching actual strippers just sit there quietly with hard-ons. They do not squeal.

Women are still, or again, very male-centered. They still ape their oppressors. They still feel deeply unsafe and disoriented when engaged in a non-male-sanctioned activity.

Plus I'd been to the original Girls' Nights Out, thank you very much. We called them consciousness-raising groups. They were the greatest mind-altering experience a woman could have. *Much* better than mescaline. A consciousness-raising group in the early seventies was an evening of unconditional support punctuated by searing insights. We ate fondue and realized we didn't have to be a servant class if we didn't want to. It was, okay, it was *liberating*. Once we were talking about masturbation and . . . no, never mind, it's still none of your business. Suffice it to say it could not be anything like this nineties version.

But I went anyway. It was not at all what I expected. Except for the outfits. We were all glamorous, impeccably sophisticated visions. For men we just try to look skinnier so they won't think we have a ginormous butt or anything, for women we pull out all the stops because let's face it, is a guy gonna know that the black velvet number with a standing boat neckline and taffeta frills around the hem is actually a work of art? Men don't even know what clothes are called. They think everything that isn't pants is a *dress*, for God's sake. I personally got up four times to twirl around the room to be admired by my eagle-eyed peers.

But there were no single women on the prowl pretending not to be. Instead I found myself in a group of enormously tired women who were trying to be supportive companions to their men, nurturing mothers and successful career women. Married women.

Married women are most in need of Girls' Night Out. Tell a husband you're going to dinner with women friends and either he just assumes he's invited or sulks because what the hell is *he* supposed to eat? But tell him you're going to Girls' Night Out and he gets a fond, condescending gleam in his eye. A husband assumes just what I'd assumed, that it's really all about them.

We talked politics, art, gossip. We argued about whether Kitty should wean or not. We stuffed ourselves with bread and wine and many of us put our heads down on the table for a little nap. Men were somehow not mentioned.

At first I felt all pompous. I was an independent woman, and all my nights are girls' nights out, even if there are guys around. We never bothered labeling it, it was a way of life, and a mighty good one at that.

Then I went all wistful. Was this independence I had carved

for myself really mighty good? Wasn't I just sublimating with freedom and career my real needs for a husband and child? Wait a minute, I had a child. A husband then? Was I jealous?

No, I wasn't. Every one has an albatross around her neck. And as the evening progressed and we got more and more relaxed (plastered), those feelings of warm and supportive sisterhood rose up within us and we started carousing. It can still happen, even in the nineties.

Wrong Again

I'm lost when it comes to the status of the backlash. There was feminism and a male backlash against feminism then a feminist backlash against the male backlash and now there seems to be, correct me if I'm wrong, a male backlash against the feminist backlash.

My head is swimming. As a feminist, do I like men now, do they like me? Should we just commence to tear each other's throats out? Or is it time for a meaningful dialogue? Here's the biggest question of all:

Whose fault is it anyway?

The entire country is alive with the sound of whining. Feminists have been doing it for years, it is my movement's least attractive attribute. We tend to blame men for everything in a sniveling, wimpy sort of way. When someone backs us into a corner we sink to the floor and whimper. It's pathetic.

Now men are doing it, which is at least as unappealing. I was reading this men's magazine today, and it was full of torment: What if someone accuses us of acquaintance rape? Why do we have to know how to cook and stuff? What about our rights as fathers? What about our rights as men? Why do we always feel like walking wallets? Why are feminists such ballbusters? Why do women tell us that everything we do is wrong?

Here's a riddle: **Q:** How many masculinists does it take to screw in a lightbulb? **A:** That's not funny.

Guys, masculinists, sweat-lodge devotees, please for your own sakes lighten up. You're gonna give yourselves heart attacks. We're not listening to you anyway.

When I hear men complaining about their lot in life my stomach goes into a big angry knot while all the injustices perpetrated against women boil up inside my brain: Ah, so you don't want to be accused of acquaintance rape, do you? Well, buddy, how do you think it feels to *be* acquaintance-raped? You don't want to cook? For how many centuries were we expected to do every lick of housework? Your rights as fathers? How come so many of you never stick around long enough to claim them? Men's rights? Do me a fucking favor! Walking wallet? Well, who has all the money? Ballbusters? Who has all the balls? Everything you do *is* wrong.

Then men hear this kind of stuff and *their* stomachs knot up and they attack. Then women go insane because we're being *once again* attacked by men. And nobody listens to anybody and everybody goes off and sulks in a corner and no one at all gets laid.

What with this unholy progression of blame and counterblame, the frustration level between the sexes has shot totally off the graph.

I propose we all just stop in mid-sentence. No more whining on either side. A person who whines is a person who might actually be enjoying his (or her) martyrdom, because if it didn't satisfy him, somehow he'd stop whining and do something. But whining precludes action. Whining is as cozy as flypaper. Whining freezes you into victim status and makes you really unpopular at cocktail parties.

There is this new trend in feminism—antivictim feminism. A bunch of young whippersnappers decry the old-guard feminists for seeing themselves as victims. I want to hit them. Many women *are* victims. So are many men. Society loves to punish its victims: Welfare mothers, gays, blacks, the poor. I say punish the whiners, not the victims. Praise the victims for not going insane, especially the victims who pull themselves out of the gutter of abuse and fight back against their oppressors.

There is a fabulous irony about this battle between men and women. We are both on the same side. Okay, you can stop laughing now. We both have big problems with traditional relationships—where men are the heads of the households and control the fates of their women.

What are men's main whines? That women take them for a ride, take them to the cleaners, bleed them dry. That they must have a Porsche and a decent stock portfolio to even approach the batter's box. That men feel like a meal ticket without rights. That in the event of a divorce, the woman will get the house, car, even his kids, while a man lives on Chinese takeout in a furnished studio apartment, paying for it all.

What are women's whines? That men perceive women as having less intrinsic value than themselves. That glass ceilings prevent them from getting the good jobs. That women are always responsible for the housework and child care, and only rich women can afford cleaners and day care. That women are constantly being patronized, bullied, even sexually harassed. That their bodies are not their own, and when those bodies wear out, they'll be unceremoniously dumped for a younger model.

Men don't want to be success objects, women don't want to be sex objects. We both want to eschew traditional relationships for something more newfangled and equal. But there's a teensy snag.

Even as men complain that all women want to be taken care of, they still are loath to relinquish one iota of control either in relationships or in the workplace. And as women complain that men demand total control, they still expect men to be completely responsible for them.

We all want it both ways. It won't work. We must make sacrifices.

Men must give up ruling the roost and let the little woman get big and strong. There must be no complaints when dinner is late or nonexistent, if dark roots show and the occasional leg is unwaxed. Your mate may no longer be a glorified concubine, but she'll share your burdens and won't bleed you dry. If a woman demands that you become a prince on a white charger, *just say no*.

Women must stop wheedling and manipulating their men when they want a new sofa. We may not pout and toss our curls like little girls who need Daddy's permission or use sex as a power tool, we must be prepared to shoulder equal burdens or sacrifice all rights to equal opportunities. If a mate demands that we impersonate an inflatable doll, *just say "Blow me."*

Power Envy

I am trying to figure out how to start this thing. How about this:
Do you know how many women have been genitally mutilated in Africa? Does it make the front page of any newspaper ever? Does anybody, any man, even care? (No, no. Way too combative, guilt-tripping. Plus probably a lot of men *do* care, and just like me, they sit staring into space trying to figure out what to do about it. Go to Africa with an attitude? Then what?)

Okay, maybe this:

We live in a society where violence against women is practiced incessantly. Statistically, violent crimes have gone down, except for the rape and murder of guess who, which have increased by about 10 percent in the last decade. And if that's not scary enough, violence against women is ritualized in the media. Every week brings us a new woman-in-jeopardy-of-being-maimed-and-mutilated movie, a new rap song about tying the bitch whore to a chair and beating the shit out of her.

(Even worse! More guilt-tripping! Men will just get defensive, and when men get defensive, testosterone takes over their brains and they either become pinched and monosyllabic or throw a lamp at you. And anyway two wrongs don't make a right.)

Dammit. How can I explain how pissed off I am about the Lorena Bobbitt phenomenon without it turning into a war of the sexes, which I personally think it isn't?

Perhaps I should start by discussing women and penises.

We have no envy. I don't care what that misguided patriarch Sigmund Freud said. We may like a penis, but we don't want one. We watch men on hot days adjusting their scrotums, trying to get comfortable, and we're pleased by the state of our tidy genitalia.

Plus the idea of having to deal with penile function is terrifying. How come men can always, or almost always, get it up? Women cannot begin to fathom this. To be sexually aroused, we need everything just right. A little too much aftershave, a bad fart joke, red satin boxer shorts, the mood is ruined.

So you can keep your penises. We're happy to enjoy them but have no interest in their care and maintenance. What we do envy is your power.

Power to walk down the street at night without contorting your body to make sure it looks as purposeful and asexual as possible. Power to walk alone into a bar or restaurant without being swept head to toe with appraising eyes. The power of old-boy networks. The power of money. The power of muscles.

"Their penises are their most vulnerable part," said Cleo. "Everything about the penis makes men insecure. So we spend all our time building it up for them, telling them what a big deal it is and everything. I think we went too far."

We sure did. Women colluded with men in turning the penis into a monster. We've pointed out skyscrapers, guns, trains, things of massive power, and said, "How phallic!" You thought we meant it when we were just being pleasant and accommodating in that dreadful way that women are. We've helped you mythologize the penis, make it into a symbol of this massive power, and therefore by extension making men into symbols of massive power.

I was once up for a job on a battle-of-the-sexes kind of talk show, and was given a list of show topics from the producers. At the top of the list was "The Penis: Do women give it the respect it deserves?"

What the *fuck* does that mean? Why should we give penises any more respect than, oh, earlobes? Are we supposed to worship it, revere it, make it into some kind of mystical being? Do women demand that men pay homage to their ovaries? Come to think of it, why don't they?

That's what I said to the producer. Funnily enough, I didn't get the job.

Lorena Bobbitt is the most inanely accommodating woman in the world. An old-fashioned, man-respecting, family-oriented kind of girl without much brain. She believes in old-fashioned values. That's why she cut off her husband's dick.

Your modern, nineties kind of a feminist is not steeped in the mythology of male power residing in the genitalia. Your modern woman believes in equality. But an old-fashioned girl believes she is inferior to her husband, believes she should steal some pretty dresses to make herself as attractive as she can because she is powerless without him, identifies so strongly with her man that she feels she has no identity at all if she separates from him, which is why she doesn't just pick up and leave when he rapes and abuses her.

An old-fashioned girl identifies so strongly with her man that she even identifies with his fantasies and fears. A big fear men have is *vagina dentata,* a vagina with teeth that will bite their penises right off. Supposedly this has something to do with overbearing mothers, but whatever, it's very annoying. We have no interest in biting off or severing the penis from the body in any way. Except for Lorena Bobbitt, who has so little independent substance that she took her husband's fears as her own. We call it identifying with the oppressor.

So anyway, if one more man throws Lorena Bobbitt at me and says, "There's feminism for you!" I will froth at the mouth.

Too many men, noticeably media men, are always on the lookout to discredit feminism. In the eighties they trotted out Andrea Dworkin, a very strange fringe feminist who says all penetration is rape, and tried to get the world to believe that she was the feminist role model, that all feminists were identical twins with Andrea. Now they're trying the same thing with Lorena Bobbitt, a woman who should be the poster child for obsessive-compulsive maniacs.

Even poor befuddled Lorena said, If you're like me, get help. She didn't say, Hey gals, let's go on a dick-severing rampage!

Freud was right about one thing. It's called transference. Look it up.

Ode to Sweatpants

When I was a baby I wore comfy stretch suits. Then everything went downhill. Organdy dresses. Scratchy sweaters. Sanitary belts.

And here's one thing I can't believe I ever had on my body:

THE PANTY GIRDLE

"I'm going to count to three," my mother would menace, "and you'd better have that thing on, little miss!"

Yeah sure. Count to three thousand, bitch. First I had to unravel the thing, then it would be inside out, then I'd unravel it the other way, it would still be inside out, then I'd give up and shove a leg in and pull. And pull and pull and pull and pull and finally get the bastard up to my waist, although the crotch was still below my knees. Then it was time to put on those hideous burnt-orange stockings that ran and ran and ran. Then after a screaming tirade from my mother about bankruptcy caused by inordinate burnt-orange stocking purchases two unblemished stockings would finally be fastened into the rubber-and-steel contraptions called garters, cutting into my thighs and creating really lovely bulges of flesh and accordion pleats at the ankles that I would try to eradicate by grabbing the toe, tucking any extra fabric under my feet, and then try to walk, ignoring that bound-foot feeling and the gangrene developing in my waist and thighs, and never even *think* about peeing.

That didn't last long, only from eleven to thirteen. Then it was time for a fresh horror:

HIGH-HEELED SHOES

Right, they make your butt jut out saucily and your ankles lose that elephantine quality, but at what price?

At first they feel kind of okay. Then your toes tingle. Then your little toe, thrust forward into the shoe's point, starts rubbing against the side and a blister forms. Then that muscle in your foot's arch spasms. Then your toes go completely numb. Then your toes come back to life in dire pain. Then another blister forms where the shoe has been cutting into the back of your foot. Then you can't walk at all, take five aspirin, fall over and sprain both ankles.

I phased out high heels ten years ago. I will wear them again the same time I decide to, what the hell, go bungee jumping.

One thing I was loath to give up:

GARTER BELTS

Stockings got stretchy, eliminating thigh bulges and ankle wrinkles, metal garters were transformed to easy-snap plastic, and okay, there was occasional numbness where the thing cut into the hips, but this was a minor annoyance compared to the male-lust-enhancing qualities of these lace and elastic confections.

But how many times can I put the damned things on without déjà vu? And how come most of the men who demand them are so cavalier about monogamy? And what about that rampaging story about the guy who kept a bag of different-sized and -styled garter belts under his bed as he tried to seduce every woman in Manhattan? And, please, enough with Victoria's Secret. How sexy can a garter belt be when I no longer have to prowl the East Village, but just pop over to any mall? Plus the clothes dryer, when tired of socks, eats them. Another dinosaur:

DRESSES

Dresses are for ladies. I never go to afternoon bridge parties or Broadway openings, I am no lady. Dresses think they make a statement, but I am no longer willing to let my clothing speak for me, since it never learned how to say, "You are very boring, please go away," at cocktail parties. Women who wear fur coats love dresses. Plus with dresses I have to wear

PANTY HOSE

And sometimes, when I'm feeling fat (okay, all the time) control-top panty hose.

I pull them up, they snap down, I pull them up again, they rip. When I try to put them on after a shower they stick to my skin and fight me to the death. When I finally think I've won, when I give those suckers that final tug that pulls them up around the waist, the crotch rips apart, which I try to get away with but soon the runs that start at the ripped crotch snake right down to my toes.

SKIRTS

See panty hose, above.

JEANS

Great, right? Utilitarian. Can be dressed up, or down.

Unless I've just had a big dinner and the waistband and zipper pops open the moment I stand up, as invariably happens when I'm trying to affect a steely dignity.

Also they come out of the dryer any size they want to be. I put them on, they're too tight, I scream, run to the scale, false alarm. I put them on, they're nice and loose, I jump on the scale, throw off my shoes and watch and rings, and still I've gained two pounds.

Jeans, I've decided, are only for very dressy events. Weddings. Otherwise, it's

SWEATPANTS

Ooh la la! I wear them at night, in the morning, I jump out of bed, voilà, I'm dressed!

Sweatpants are appropriate for every occasion, if you don't mind having a humongous butt, which I find I don't. I wore them the other night to an AIDS benefit where others were in gowns and tails, I fit right in.

Plus they're comfy and stretchy. Now I just need a crib back!

The Scare of Solohood

I am so lonely I could die. I wake up in the morning, realize I don't have a boyfriend, and put my head in the oven. I go to the supermarket, fill my cart with Lean Cuisine servings for one, am too demoralized to let the cashier see the pathetic contents of my cart, slink away. I go to parties, night classes, museums, various clubs and mixers with my eyelashes curled hopefully, am wracked with disappointment to find only more hopeful women with curly eyelashes. I go to dinner parties, my throat seizes up with envy watching the happy couples who are my friends. My nights are long with longing.

Also I have a very large bridge in New York to sell you. Ho ho ho.

I am so goddamned sick of the myth, the stereotype of the unattached woman. Like none of us have anything better to do than pine away. Like right now I've got to go feed and play with a fifteen-year-old dog named Mabel whose human has been in the hospital for months. Mabel, with her old streaming eyes and her stiff careful walk, used to be the life and soul of Montana, traveling miles each day to romp with friends at all her designated farms. But now she's stuck in a little apartment in Santa Monica, staring into space, waiting, solo.

Solo! The new word of the moment! I pick up *TV Guide* or *People* and my eye doesn't have to stray more than a millimeter to read this dread word. Some young starlet is again SOLO and whimpering wistfully about why she can never get it right (because you're a wimp with cotton candy expectations, airhead!). Some older starlet, bravely facing down an alcoholic abusive marriage, is grimly but hopefully SOLO (tell it to Betty Ford, doll!).

Solo is even worse than its predecessor, *single*. *Single* means sweaty, tawdry, reeking with halitosis, on the make. *Solo* is doom, gloom, anxiety and alienation. *Solo* is the nineties version of single.

And so far, in all my perusals of tabloid journalism, I have never even once seen the word *solo* applied to a man. I am sure you are shocked by this. No, me neither.

I do not blame men for this, I blame a warped and entropic society that needs to have women in thrall to men to keep its precarious status quo. We are hierarchical, we need a servant class. Women, African Americans, Hispanics keep the wheels greased and the beds made.

Solo is a scare tactic. It virtually shouts to women, "Be afraid! Be very afraid! You must be part of a couple or you'll be miserable! You must stop this independence nonsense and any sort of eccentricity! Join the gang! Don't make trouble! Quick, throw on some high heels and a G-string before you're too old and *solo forever!*"

This is not to say that there was a minuscule period in my life, maybe only from 1978 to 1983, when I was a jangled, groveling, beseeching, desperate little lump of a girl with big needs. BIG needs. My whole life paled before the fact that I didn't have a guy. There was no taste in my mouth, I had no reflection in my mirror. Having a boyfriend would make me whole, I thought. Hell, having a boyfriend would make me *exist*. This is what propaganda ingrained since birth will do to the tender female psyche. I am sick to death of the propaganda and of the word *solo*.

I have just got back from visiting Mabel. She's perking up. She no longer walks to the gate, sees that it's closed, walks away four steps, forgets that the gate is closed, walks back, sees that it's closed, turns around, forgets, turns, forgets. Maybe it's all the cuddles I'm giving her, or maybe the Prozac.

"Aren't we just the nicest?" I said to my friend Lynn Ann, who's sharing Mabel duties.

"Somebody has to do it," she said. And she's right. You can't let a sweet old girl like Mabel pace frantically in a kennel. She's devoted her life to being devoted.

What I've done with my life, since I got over my own self-imposed frantic pacing and waiting for the thunderbolt of romance, is to open it up. Love my friends, rescue old dogs. I'll never match Mabel for devotion, but still.

Lynn Ann came with me to the dentist yesterday, held my hand and joked around while they pulled out a tooth that was impacted up to my nose. This I figure is the point of life, to have friends like Lynn Ann in it. Or Ed, or Eileen, Steven, Merrill, Maggie. I have an embarrassment of riches. When the phone rings and it's Lynn Ann, I'm happy.

Being *solo* means if the phone rings and it's not a guy, then whoever it is is of diminished importance. Being *solo* means that your friends, all the people who give form and function to your life, are just a way station until that perfect mate comes along.

You know those people who disappear whenever they've met a new prospect? How we resent them for making us feel disposable and devalued? Those people also give me the heebie-jeebies, they emit this scary metallic vibe of isolation. Pacing and frantic. They live in a tiny kennel in their heads. Even during their disappearing act when they think they've met somebody they're still alone, because the mate is too symbolic. A mate means security, status. A mate is a commodity.

Mabel's human called me yesterday, a very depressed hospital patient.

"Before I went into the hospital I thought everything was okay," she said. "But now I feel so totally alone. Nobody visits me. The fact that I'm in the hospital makes absolutely no difference in anyone's life, nobody's upset or inconvenienced. Not that I want anyone upset or inconvenienced, but you know what I mean. I want to be loved and needed."

"People love you, you're just depressed because you've been in the hospital so long," I said, but my heart went out to her.

No human (or dog) is an island, we need each other desperately, we need to be needed desperately. But to listen to the propaganda, to pin all our hopes and needs on husbands and wives and nuclear families is self-defeating.

To find love, give up searching. Just look right in front of you.

Dear Problem Lady:

She said she didn't mean it. She said it just happened and she doesn't know what got into her but I do.

It was Harry Finkle, a suspender-wearing son of a bitch with buffed fingernails and Italian loafers.

I don't know why she didn't just shoot me in the kneecaps instead of sleeping with that ridiculous, preening fuck. She knows how I despise him. Well, how I used to simply despise him. Now I loathe him with such a red-hot intensity I'm about to explode.

I'm not too happy with her either. I mean I guess the marriage is over. A wife doesn't cheat on her husband, especially a husband who never cheated on her. And let me tell you, there was a hot blond number in Miami last year who had quite a yen for me. She had the tiniest waist, the biggest brown eyes, a great kind of gurgling laugh, and the way her neck curved . . . I might be digressing here.

The point is, I didn't and she did. I held myself back from plain, no-frills lust whereas my beloved wife went in for grand-scale, Olympic-level dalliance.

She says it wasn't. She says they were on a business trip and it was late at night and there's always been a little sexual tension between them, which she was always ashamed of because she knows Finkle is such an asshole but they were drunk and she was lonely and a little mad at me because I don't agree she should quit her job and take one with half the salary. She knows I'm right, but it ticked her off a little and next thing we know she's in bed with fat-face.

The thing that worries me more than anything is that all those TV shrinks, etc., always say that when women cheat it's much more serious than when a man cheats, that women are biologically different and every sexual encounter with them is meaningful whereas with men we know it should always be meaningful but sometimes it's just a fuck.

You know what I wish? I wish she hadn't told me. I'd rather be blissfully ignorant of her perfidy than in this hell.

So do I call a lawyer?

Sleepless

Dear Sleepless:

No, you moron. You encourage her to get that new job.

Come on, stop your internal whining and think a minute.

She wants to quit her job. You don't like the idea. Next thing you know, she sleeps with someone she works with, someone she knows you hate with all your soul. A + B = C. She's getting back at you big-time, pal.

Do you know what it's like when you really, really hate your job, which your wife must do if she wants another one at half the salary? I hear men are able to compartmentalize these things, perhaps they can. But women go to pieces. Their whole world is permeated with gray, thudding pain. They cry in the employees' bathroom. They get nauseous even driving near their workplace. They lose their hearts, minds and self-esteem.

Okay, it would have been a lot more straightforward if she'd just said, "Fuck you, I'm quitting my job, and if you try to stop me, I'm going to go down on Harry Finkle." This would be more honest and appropriate.

But women have been propagandized from the cradle to be passive, to be accommodating, to avoid confrontation. This can be a real drag when you passionately want something and are pathologically afraid of demanding it, or even of asking nicely. So women either spend a couple of decades on a shrink's couch to learn to be vaguely assertive, or they become masterfully oblique, goddesses of manipulation.

Problem Lady

Dear Problem Lady:

I want to come out at work. No I don't. Yes I do.

Okay, I'll start from the beginning. When I met Rhoda, I didn't think of myself as a lesbian. I thought I was undersexed. I thought all those fantasies I had about women were slight aberrations that would go away as soon as I found Mr. Perfect Jewish Guy. So I kept trying.

And then came Rhoda, who lived upstairs. She was older, she was beautiful. I wanted to dress like her, talk like her, run my tongue over my upper lip when I was watching TV like her. One day she invited me up for a cocktail party. I was the only one there. I thought I'd died and gone to heaven.

This was three years ago, and Rhoda has long since broken my heart, the bitch. But she taught me who I was.

But she didn't teach me how to tell people. I'd been a practicing heterosexual for so long! I would sit around with my friends from work and talk about which men were cute, which were bastards, which had problems with castrating mothers. My life was totally male-oriented, because I had been taught from birth to be that way. Okay, I've told my mother. She thought I was kidding around. She finally believes it. Although you can't stop her from introducing me to "eligible" men.

But how will I tell the people at work? I'm so enmeshed with everyone there, I couldn't stand it if they started acting funny around me. The women and I still talk about men, the boss still flirts with me. I've been at the firm for ten years, it's all very comfortable.

And yet not. I've always thought the term "living a lie" was pure soap opera, but that's what I'm doing, and it's giving me ulcers. Please help.

L.D.

Dear L. D.:

You have to tell them. All the time you don't, you're living negatively; as soon as you do, you'll start living positively. The relief will bring tears to your eyes.

If you're nervous, just tell the person you like best and she can tell everyone else.

Okay, here's the hard part. You have to be normal and jokey and open about it. You have to talk about your dates: where you went, what she said, what you said, whether you're in love.

If you're embarrassed and defensive, your friends will be too. They'll be frightened to say anything in case they offend you, in case they're not being PC enough . . .

You can't be afraid of them judging you, because *they're* afraid you're judging *them* for being so silly and weak and in thrall to the power of men. Women heterosexuals feel that way all the time, and being around a lesbian can exacerbate these feelings.

Your boss will still flirt with you. He may even step it up, what with all those new fantasies about you he's got playing in his head.

It will be okay, and if it isn't, you don't want to work there anyway. And you never know, they might already know.

Problem Lady

Looking for a Life

Coyotes Are Laughing

*F*irst of all, I would like to thank my ex-house. If it had not unrelentingly made life a living hell, if it had not stepped up its efforts in recent weeks by hiding things, moving things, pretending to leak gas and generally wreaking havoc so that there was no choice but to move, the dogs and I would now be buried under rubble. I moved to West L.A. exactly one week before the earthquake. I had only to contend with a carpet of broken glass.

(Oh God, the house just rocked big-time. I turned on NBC. "Yes, we just had another aftershock," some guy said, then they went back to Zsa Zsa hawking her exercise video on Phil.)

Anyway, the earthquake woke me and I remember thinking, "Okay, fine, that was wonderful, all right already, we're all very impressed, really majestic, thank you, now cut it out." It finally stopped and I thought, "That's it, I've got to get out of this town," and turned on the light. "Damn, the bulb's out," I thought and counted a full complement of dogs lumped together on the bed.

"I jumped up and ran around my apartment like a rabid pony," Steven said. "I ran ten miles in circles in one minute."

"I woke up screaming," said Susan.

"I wouldn't move, they had to come in and get me," said Elizabeth.

I don't remember much. Just flashes. Crunching across glass to the sound of splashing water in the kitchen. Scary bursts of light outside, which turned into a man holding a flashlight peering in my window.

"Are you all right?" he asked. We'd never met, but I knew he was the hippie-Buddhist from next door. "Do you have a flashlight?"

"Was that like a *big* earthquake?" I asked. "Oh yeah," he said, and gave me his flashlight and told me to get in my car in case of aftershocks. I kind of remember chasing Homer down the street, but I really came to sitting in my car, listening to a shrink on the radio trying to calm everybody down while talking to my son on the car phone.

The hippie and the guy across the street came to say "Hi" and turned off my water main.

"In my neighborhood a whole phalanx of middle-aged men patrolled their brains out, knocking on doors, turning off every water and gas main they could find," said Matt.

"In my apartment building nobody even opened their doors," said Carlene.

Then both hippies, man and wife, came and called their mothers on my car phone. We became best friends. Then I called my ex-mother-in-law. I heard on the radio that the freeways had collapsed. Then I waited until dawn so I could go into the house and sweep up glass.

Then my kitchen phone rang. It was my mother, whom I don't speak to. "Cyn, I'm fat as a pig," she said.

Then my landladies arrived whining. "All our crystal is smashed, our new house is cracked, why did we ever move?" Then they picked up my phone, waited thirty seconds for a dial tone, and called their mothers. Then it turned out I was the only one whose gas was still on, so in moments my entire house was filled with previously unknown neighbors who brought empty mugs, which I filled with coffee, and a gaggle of kids playing with the dogs.

It was very festive until they all left and I started to shake. I called everyone I knew in the Valley but couldn't get through. I took the dogs, filled the car with bottled water and food, went to my son's house because he had power so I could watch TV. We were all giddy. We watched the "Quake-Cam," the needle going crazy after each aftershock. "It's like watching the Yule log," my son said. Then his roommates went out looking for flashlights and came back disheveled, panting and flashlightless. "Everybody at Savon was fighting and screaming at each other, we're lucky to be alive!"

"At Ralph's the employees were just holding up bags of groceries and yelling 'twenty dollars!' " said Eileen.

"Can you imagine? Two dollars for a banana," said Dennis.

The few people I finally got through to in the Valley were in shock. Becky's toilet moved across the floor, she had no water, no power, no gas, no back wall. Pam's husband had seizured. A friend told me that Elizabeth was staying with her five kids at the Salvation Army.

My power came back on and I watched TV and shook for the next two days. During every aftershock the dogs come running at me.

"Every aftershock I think I'm going to die," Steven said.

"Every aftershock the house falls down a little more," Pam said.

"I start feeling okay and then another aftershock comes and I'm rigid with fear," Mike said.

TV didn't get annoying until Thursday, when the real news got slow for a moment and they started trotting out movie stars showing us their rubble.

Just like my ex-house, I'm thinking Los Angeles is trying to give humans a little hint. I feel like I've spent the past two years watching fires destroying structures. Riots upon floods upon fires upon earthquakes. The land doesn't care. It pays absolutely no attention to people like that poor deluded guy on the news who said, "It's inexcusable for people not to have homes!" Humans can feel all the entitlement they want, nature is implacable. This last earthquake was just the mountains deciding to get bigger.

Maybe we should give the city back to the rattlesnakes and coyotes before they take it by force.

Where to Live: A Shopping Spree (1)

*L*ike all artistic types who ran screaming from identically stultifying suburbs to the big city a couple of decades ago, I'm now
trying to figure out where to live.

Is there anywhere we could all go to? Where there isn't green
slime in the gutters? Where no crazed crackheads routinely hold
guns to our heads? Anywhere with a little peace and a few trees but
with a marked absence of deer-huntin', double-knit-wearin',
queer-hatin', Bible-totin', Quayle-missin' bigots? Where a person
could have a dog or so and see a movie besides *Jurassic Park*?

My publishers think I'm on a book tour. But in fact I'm on a
sixteen-city shopping spree to find a new place to live. Come along.

Our first stop is **Los Angeles.** We can't live here. They chew
up artistic types and spit their bones into the La Brea Tar Pits. You
don't even have to go out looking for a job to get smashed in the
teeth. You can be curled up at home reading murder mysteries
when someone from, say, *The Paula Poundstone Show* phones to
ask if you'd like a job, and when you go down there they make you
sit for forty-five minutes without so much as a "Want some coffee?," just long enough to notice the other writers look like suicidal

rabbits, when the producer, someone named Bonnie who thinks she's quite fabulous, finally appears, looks at you, and says, "Oh. I thought you were some other writer I really like."

Even Bible-thumpers are more fun than this.

There is a certain cozy seediness and surfeit of big affable guys in plaid shirts in **Toronto.** Several inhabitants sport nice outfits and make sharply humorous remarks. There's cute money. Plus there's free health care, paid for by cigarettes costing six dollars a pack. And everybody smokes like fiends, which is endearing.

But they want to be New York. They spend a lot of time telling you that Margaret Atwood is the best writer in the world. And if you're going to leave the country, why not go somewhere exotic, like nuclear-free New Zealand?

Then again, how long would it take *Angels in America* to get to New Zealand? Oh, God.

Maybe **New York** is the only place. It has *Angels.* It has bookstores like Three Lives, Wendell's, and Rizzoli. It has Harold Wise, M.D., the only doctor in the country who knows enough to tell you to take acidophilus with your antibiotics. It has that ever-popular attitude.

But that famous green slime is no longer content to stay in the gutters. Now it travels through the actual air. After walking four blocks down Seventh Avenue I was covered with the stuff. Plus I have discovered that to be a successful New Yorker you must always be in a state of rage just a quarter degree from overboiling.

You can live in **Philadelphia** only if cheese steaks are your singular passion in life.

If you go to a ball game in **Boston,** even a *basketball* game, you will only see white people in the audience.

Although **Washington, D.C.,** is a city that alternates only between marble buildings and ghettos, you're right in the middle of some serious action. I could feel the electricity even from my room in the Wyndham Hotel, a hotel you must never stay in if you value your sanity.

"Don't live here. Washington is a city without a soul," said a very smart and attractive man with a smart and attractive shirt who hung around after I did a reading and in fact took me out to dinner.

"It's a city of transients, a city with no personality," he said the next day as he unpacked a care package of vitamin C, chamomile tea, garlic-parsley tablets and special honey he had brought me to take care of my raging head cold. "You can't even predict how people are going to drive, and if you don't work for the government, there's no point."

"Oh, okay," I said, secretly wondering where else I would find smart guys in smart shirts who would make me chamomile care packages after knowing me for only twenty-four hours.

Cleveland is a really nice town. It's got lots of parks and beautiful old houses, even an artsy-craftsy-groovy-Soho-ish part of town. The people are nice, well-read, pleasant. You can find a Bakelite napkin-holder for eight dollars, an art-movie theater or two, and plenty of good bookstores. But it's *Cleveland*, for God's sake.

Ditto **Dayton.**

I was thinking maybe **Chicago.** I really was. Lots of trees, lots of dogs, a beach right in the middle of town. Art museums, theaters, you want it, you got it.

But the Bulls just won the finals. I'm looking down from my seventeenth-story hotel window onto one hundred thousand men rampaging in the streets. They are punching the air with their fists. They are doing the Arsenio yodel. They have taken their shirts off. They are pouring beer over one another. They are dancing atop cars. They are mooning each other.

Seven cities to go.

Where to Live:
A Shopping Spree (2)

*I*f any author tells you how much she hates doing book tours, how tiring they are, how she has to keep answering the same goddamned dumb questions over and over again, just smack her.

A writer on a book tour is the Queen of the World. In each city, her publisher provides a personal nursemaid who opens doors, feeds her, takes her to every single vintage clothing shop. Plus there are bookshop owners, concierges, bellhops and publicists who pretend she is the most important, most beautiful person ever. So what that she has to wake up some mornings at five to do drive time?

In other words, I'm home from my tour and depressed. I pick up the phone to call room service for a club sandwich and all I get is a dial tone or a son who growls, "Get it yourself, I'm going to the beach." There are stacks of bills and stacks of dogs. I am in actual tears to be back in this hell that is Los Angeles. Get me outta here.

Okay, this is part 2, where were we? I was using the book tour as a shopping spree to find us all a new place to live. We're very picky, we've discarded New York, L.A., Chicago, Philadelphia,

Washington, D.C., Toronto, Boston, Cleveland and Dayton. Let's try **Minneapolis.**

You know, it's really great here! Green, riddled with gorgeous lakes. Smart, ridiculously nice people except for my one lone stalker who isn't even that scary. Incredible bookstores, including a mystery bookstore where you can tell them a vague memory ("The heroine wears an ugly purple scarf") and they'll find the book. The ex-wife of the governor has a radio show here, and she's happy to discuss her black dildo (at length). You can pretend to be Mary Richards and throw your hat up in the air.

You just have to not mind ten months of serious winter.

Want to feel like you've just landed on the cover of a Jane Smiley novel? Go to **Iowa City.**

Well, fly to Cedar Rapids and drive through astonishingly beautiful country to get to this tiny college town with one wonderful bookstore, lots of bars where frat boys get drunk, and an enormous Hardee's, which I believe may be some variant of McDonald's. We can go there for the college's writer's program, but we'll have to live somewhere else.

Not **Dallas.** All Texans say that Dallas isn't really Texas, that it's too far east and too full of big hair. So why be in Texas if you're not really in Texas?

Austin! Yeah! Great music scene! An arty-creative college/ state government town! Full of beauty and eccentricity!

I always thought I would eventually live in Austin. Something in the warm soft air cradled me, filled me with desire and a sense of possibility. Imagine my disappointment when I discovered Austin is dead.

If not dead, co-opted. The evocative old downtown area has been ripped to shreds and filled with towering Hyatts, etc. The music scene, which everyone thought would explode the way Seattle's did, has become crabby and cutthroat. Sixth Street is full of sordidly meandering drunks. Everyone who hasn't moved away is feeling alienated and depressed, although they eat spectacular food while they whine.

Maybe it's just me, but I have never gotten **San Francisco.** I know it's supposed to be so gorgeous and all, but where? I *do* know fabulously adventurous babes there. And okay, there's a guy and whenever we see each other we rip each other's clothes off even when we promise we won't.

While I was there I was watching TV, which was soon drowned out by sirens, and I thought, "Hey, this is just like New York, maybe I do like it here." But then it turned out to be just some sniper picking off lawyers a couple of blocks away.

"It's just a mean shitty little place for people who don't have to work," says my friend Jake, who hates everything, "rich liberals with a holier-than-thou attitude."

He wants attitude? He should try **Seattle.** They *must* get over themselves. First there was the groovy theater scene. Then *Twin Peaks.* Then the grunge thing. Now the movie, which has turned their heads so far I expect them to start spouting pea soup. Last year I stayed at the Sorrento Hotel. They couldn't have been more adorable and attentive, giving me little treats and matchboxes with my actual name engraved on them. This year it was like, "Are you sure you are hip enough to stay in this fabulous hotel?"

The whole city was permeated with this attitudinous vibe, which is okay for New Yorkers, but not okay for a bunch of boring people whose biggest quest in life is finding the best latte.

I worried about **Portland** (Oregon) when I scanned the Yellow Pages. There are as many Christian bookstores as holistic, crystal-type places. And their pet-shop ads say, "We buy mixed-breed dogs," which, since I know how hard it is to find homes for mixed breeds, filled me with dreadful suspicions involving research labs. (I called them all. They only buy puppies and sell them for eighty dollars to morons.)

If you're nostalgic for an old-fashioned, us-against-the-assholes, left vs. right kind of fight, rush right here. The ultra–politically correct are constantly butting heads with antigay, anti–spotted owl rednecks. It's charming. Plus I found the Mecca of vintage clothing stores, Ray's Ragtime.

We should all move there now before somebody makes a movie called *Pacing in Portland* and ruins everything.

Where to Live, Part 3

$\mathcal{S}$hit, shit, shit. It may have to be Portland or Hoboken after all. When I was looking around the country for a new place to live, a place that wasn't New York or L.A., where you could have a couple of trees but a minimum of Jew- and queer-hating Bible-thumping rednecks, I thought I had an ace in the hole.

England used to be such a lovely country. Small, green, eccentric. You could live in a village, in Oxfordshire, say, where artists, builders, poets, pig farmers and TV writers were all part of the same gang. You could walk on deserted little paths lousy with hedgerows and pheasants and assorted greenery and bring your dog into the pub. Then when you got bored with that you could hop on a train and in an hour be in London, which was bustling and big but safe and riddled with crooked lanes and goofy shops and everywhere you went everyone was polite and madly witty and you were not only allowed but actually encouraged to be just as peculiar as you could ever want. True, there were drab gray men and people who adored Margaret Thatcher running around, but anyone who was anyone just pretended there weren't.

Plus, and this was really crucial, crazy old bats were rampant.

You couldn't turn a corner without bumping into some old babe in a fedora and cape carrying a stick, trailed by five spaniels. No double-knit polyester, no horrible little cement hairdos, no furtive "I'm sorry, I realize I'm not supposed to exist anymore" facial expressions. And not only did the English respect these old bats but they actually spoke to them as if they were human beings and not terrifying symbols of mortality.

But it's all gone horribly wrong. England now sucks.

The day I got here on my biyearly visit, Germaine Greer went on television and destroyed crazy old batitude. She wore a schoolboy's outfit and whined about "youthism." She blamed it on the baby boomers, being so individualistic and self-absorbed and all. Said she wants to grow old disgracefully. It was a transparent temper tantrum about not being sexy anymore. Germaine has made all present and future old bats self-conscious and ashamed and she's ruined everything.

Even worse, the drab gray men have taken over. Margaret Thatcher's memoirs top the best-seller list. The people have finally succumbed to their hideously repressive government. Nobody has any fight left in them. Or even brains.

For instance, even last year they used to just hate hate hate Americans. We were scum—our television, our bad taste, our pretending to have morals when we were in fact greedy, bullying dickheads.

This was irritating enough, but now they have *become* Americans. Well sort of. I'm in England right now, and it's kind of like being in an alternate universe where George Bush won the 1992 presidential elections.

The Tory government has just had this conference, where they shoved family values down the throats of the populace. FAMILY FUCKING VALUES! Single mothers are evil! Also the cause of all this escalating crime! Welfare cheats are bleeding the country dry!

This is all fine, they have to say this shit, they're desperate.

They used to say, "Look how rich we're making you!" but now they're in a deep recession. And they can't say, "Thatcherism has raped, bankrupted and destroyed our country and turned people insane, suicidal and criminal, but can't we still be in power anyway?" They have to blame the victim, it's only fair.

But the moronic victims are lapping it up. They're all nodding to each other soberly and quoting obscure "studies" that prove that most criminals emerge from single-parent families. Even the erstwhile esteemed and reliable left-wing press is spouting this drivel. And the tabloids are having a field day. Here are today's *Daily Mail* headlines: VICTORY FOR THE ABSENT FATHERS! and WELFARE CHEATS ARE COSTING THE TAXPAYERS £5BN EACH YEAR!

Then there's a date-rape brouhaha. Some guy was at a party and followed an incredibly drunk girl outside, realized she was in no fit state to return to the party, and carried her home. Then had sex with her. Said she was begging for it. She remembers nothing. He was acquitted. Now he's a national hero. Men are all walking around with patronizing smirks. Women with newspaper columns are writing this guy notes of apology. I'm just a stupid Yank, I don't get it. If he noticed that she was too plastered to return to a party or even, in fact, walk, why is he a hero for then fucking her?

Then the Labour Party, supposed to be the good guys, managed to force a few women out of government. (Don't ask me to explain, it's all boring and about shadow cabinets.) They're smirking, too. England is a repellent smirkfest.

When the Republicans tried this kind of shit we rose up as a nation and got rid of the bastards. True, our country is a fetid sinkhole ravaged by crime and assholes with Porsches and/or Bibles, but at least we happily admit it.

I'm proud to be an American.

I Opened the Window
and Influenza

If you liked the headline, you'll love the column. I am a snotfest. I have a fever of 101 degrees and counting. I have seen every movie on AMC. I am very stupid. Please don't expect the well-turned phrase or even the clever, what's it called, I know this word, segue. I sense some very awkward segues coming on. Now the word *segue* doesn't look like a word at all. Is it?

Two weeks ago I was driving around and thinking, "Wow, am I in a bad mood." Nothing failed to annoy. A woman in a green flared skirt crossed the street and I thought, "Oh, right, and I suppose that skirt is supposed to mean something deep and significant about your tedious little personality, you dork." Every time the light turned red I had a full-blown temper tantrum, punching the steering wheel and everything. Then I tried to start a New York–style traffic jam. Out here, when traffic is gridlocked, not only do they not get out of their cars and holler and punch their roofs in apoplectic fury, they don't even beep. I started beeping my horn continuously and screaming, "Come on you wimps, start beeping, show some fucking spirit, you stupid cocksuckers!"

Then "Stand by Your Man" came on the radio and I started to

sob. I went home and got into bed immediately. Turned on AMC, watched Betty Grable look for love in outfits. Went to sleep for sixteen hours with the lights on. Woke up to exactly where I came in on the Betty movie. See, she wanted to marry a rich guy and millionaire Robert Cummings was in love with her but she really loved Don Ameche but it turned out he wasn't rich and then there was her sister who was pretending to be her secretary. It was way too complicated and exhausting. I have always fancied romantic comedies, but after watching about thirty of them in a row, I've noticed they are loathsome. You know in the first five minutes who's going to end up together and then you have to sit for an hour and a half of misunderstandings and tiffs until what you knew would happen happens. Even my beloved Rosalind Russell in *Take a Letter, Darling* failed to please. She gave it all up—the job, the independence, the hats—for love. Just like Katharine Hepburn in *Woman of the Year* and every other piece of movie propaganda from the forties and fifties except for my beloved *His Girl Friday*, where she gives it all up for the job.

Then again, I also saw *Boomerang*, and except for Eddie's inch-thick makeup I thought it was damn good. I'm not well.

Five days into the sickness my housekeeper, the one who keeps bringing me her cast-off furniture, arrived on her weekly visit to change my sweaty sheets. "I see Brodie has moved out," she said.

"No, his boxes and stuff are all over the living room," I said. She forced me out of bed and into the living room. No boxes, no nothing. My son had left home again. (Yes Joyce, I'm burying the lead.)

I called him. "When did you move out?"

"Yesterday and the day before."

"Where was I?"

"You were there."

"Did you talk to me?"

"Yeah."

"Did I answer?"

"Not really, you kind of muttered."

Three days later my beloved friend from England came to see me and we went to lunch and had tea and took walks, and although every once in a while I had to put my head down for no reason, I felt pretty much okay. He had to go. I begged him not to. He went anyway. I stayed up all night, decided life wasn't worth living, it was too lonely and stupid and foreign.

The next day I decided I was suicidal and called all my friends and left tearful good-bye messages. Then I went to the doctor. (You may wonder why I didn't go to the doctor before. I hate going to the doctor because I always think I'm faking it. Our mothers live within us forever.)

The doctor told me I had not only the flu but two secondary infections. So I didn't have to kill myself after all, I just had to take antibiotics. What a relief.

This morning about 6 A.M. I woke up and saw that one of the dogs had smeared the duvet cover with what I hoped was mud. But I wasn't sure so I stumbled up, stripped off the cover, put it in the washing machine and then tried to watch TV but I couldn't find the remote control.

Then I drank three quarts of chamomile tea and wrote this column. Then I went to get the duvet cover out of the washing machine and there was the remote control, all sparkling clean.

I think I'll leave home too.

My Life as a Tank

Sunday: I just got out of the shower and I'm looking in the mirror and wondering whose body this is. It can't be mine. I would never have a body this gross. A butt as big as the Ritz. Thighs like a dirty secret. This is one repulsive body. I refuse to have it anymore. I am going on a diet.

I'll go on a diet and pretty soon I could look like Linda Hamilton in *Terminator 2* or Susan Sarandon in *Bull Durham*. Any girl in any jeans ad would be fine with me.

I want to wear jeans without scaring people, without them thinking a battleship is approaching. I want to look sexy and desirable in jeans. Not like this huge pig I see in the mirror.

Tomorrow I will go to one of those diet places. But right now I must put on a muumuu.

Monday: In my neighborhood, probably in every neighborhood in the country, there are five diet places per square mile. There are obviously quite a few fat-pig women who want to look good in jeans.

I visit three diet places and meet three greedy morons. Morons with syrupy voices who all say their diet is the only one that works because they have discovered the trick of weight loss without ever feeling hungry. You eat as much as you want. You don't even have to cook. Just pop these meals, prepared *just for you,* into your handy microwave. Every meal is super unbelievably delicious! You will lose, lose, lose! All credit cards accepted!

As a person who's been on a few diets, I know this to be a lie. You can never eat as much as you want and you always feel madly hungry. The only real trick is to take speed. I hate speed.

I run home in distress and call all my friends to find out which diet place to go to. They've all been to at least one. Cleo, Louise and Rita all say they'll go with me.

"But you're not fat," I say to Cleo, Louise and Rita.

"Are you kidding? I'm a walking office block," says Cleo.

"Oh, please, I'm a cow about to give birth," says Louise.

"I am an actual beached whale," says Rita.

I sift information and eventually wind up in a place where the diet person is not quite a moron.

"Four high-fiber crackers a day, seven ounces of protein, two teaspoons of fat, one apple and all the salad you can eat, except no carrots or tomatoes," the dietician says.

"You're fucking kidding me," I say.

"You'll lose twenty pounds in a month," she says.

"I'm your girl," I say.

I go home and start the famous prediet ritual: Eating everything I can. Cheeseburgers. Fries. Mallomars. Quite a few Mallomars. I want to throw up.

Tuesday: Please, somebody feed me. I'm going to faint. I'm starving to death.

I'm supposed to go out with a friend tonight. I call her.

"I can't go. All I can think about is food. I'm seeing spots," I say. "All day I can only eat a couple of crackers and some salad."

"You talk about salad as if it isn't food."

"Salad isn't food. Salad is slimy green background for croutons."

"All I ever eat is salad," she says.

Caught being a salad-hater, I'm humiliated. Everything makes me feel humiliated. My hugeness makes me want to hide. I know I'm perceived as weak and ridiculous. I know that all over town phones are ringing and people are saying, "I ran into Cynthia the other day. At least I think it was Cynthia. It may have been a bus, ha-ha-ha."

Wednesday: Just jumped on the scale. Haven't lost one fucking ounce.

Thursday: Not a fucking ounce.

Friday: I call Cleo. "I'm so hungry," I say. She asks what I'm eating. I tell her.

"Drink a lot of coffee. It's like speed," she pronounces.

"I'm not allowed caffeine."

Cleo hangs up on me. She hates me, too. Just because I'm fat. An hour later the doorbell rings. Cleo and Rita. A house call.

"Okay," says Rita, "how overweight do you think you are?"

"Twenty pounds."

"Fine, that means you're ten pounds overweight, because every woman alive, even little sticks like Cleo here, thinks she's ten pounds overweight. So we just lop ten off from the top. Now, why are you torturing yourself?"

"I'm not torturing myself."

"Ha," says Cleo, "you won't even let yourself drink coffee! Look, so what that you gained a couple of pounds while working on that TV show. You were stressed. A stressed woman is a woman who mainlines M&M's. Big fucking deal."

"But I hate my body."

"You stupid cow, you can't hate your body. If you hate your body, no diet will work and you'll get fatter and fatter. You have to fly in the face of a society that tells you you're hideous if you don't look like a movie star, or a beer-commercial babe, or a fashion model who is twelve years old and six feet tall, or one of those airbrushed girls in that magazine you work for. Women come in all shapes and sizes. Love your body in all its wondrous big-butt splendor."

"You don't think I'm ugly?"

"Well, the whining isn't attractive," says Rita. "Stop being so strict with yourself. Eat six crackers a day. Or eight! Drink a little coffee. This is getting really boring."

"Listen," I say, "you called yourself a beached whale. And Cleo said she was an office block."

"Oh, please," says Rita. "That's just a little recreational self-loathing a woman does so nobody thinks she's uppity."

Saturday: Drank coffee. Lost two pounds. Susan Sarandon, watch out.

The Joys of Self-Pity

DECEMBER 30

So what if I have nothing to do on New Year's Eve? So what that my best friend has found the love of her life and has actually said those most scary words, "We're just going to spend a quiet night, alone."

I have lots of things I could do. My son is having a party. Should be great, lots of kids drinking beer and puking. Plus he's so happy with his new girlfriend, it warms a mother's heart. Just looking at them gives me a sugar rush.

Then whatsername is giving a party too. Her name will come to me. Great girl. In development at Fox, I think. Talks about all sorts of Hollywood people, none of whom I know, so I can't tell if she's name-dropping or just happens to speak in italics. And they've discovered black out here in L.A.! Only twenty years late, what the hell. A party full of glossy people in black talking about Michael Ovitz. Pinch me.

So I could chat about deals or I could vomit beer.

I think about memorable New Year's Eves past. One fabulousness after another. That time Stephen, stoned on marijuana, refused to get out of the car so at midnight we sat freezing in the car watching him curl ever more tightly into a fetal ball. That time we went to the neighborhood Italian that had a sudden roach infestation. That time I went to Studio 54 in a little black dress and heels, then got a headache, went out to get a cab, walked a few more blocks, a few blocks more, then more, then some more, fended off a couple of guys who thought I was a hooker, four hours later I got home, feet in spasm, and crawled under my bed. That time we went to the opening of that fabulous new club where the music was so loud it changed our heartbeats and someone stepped on my hand, don't ask. That time my date brought his old girlfriend with him.

And way back when I was ten, my parents were having a big party, I had smuggled my dog into my bed. When I heard the cocktail-addled adults shrieking at midnight, my dog and I kissed tenderly.

That was my best New Year's.

Okay, that's what I am going to do. I am going to stay home. The ball will drop, and I will kiss Sally, Doc, Mike, Homer, Digby and Posy, my dogs. We will have a love feast.

It will really be fun. None of that desperate searching for the ultimate experience on the ultimate Saturday night. The point of New Year's Eve is to quietly commune with those who love you.

DECEMBER 31

11 A.M. "Just calling to wish you a happy new year," I say to Sammy on the phone.

"Yeah, you too, listen, I'm watching football."

"Okay, I won't keep you. By the way, what are you doing tonight?"

"Oh, some party."

12:20 P.M. "I'm going to this little dinner party, nothing special," says Cleo.

12:55 P.M. "Going to Harry's," says Merrill.

12:56 P.M. "We have reservations to see this great jazz musician," says Larry.

12:57 P.M. "I'm cooking for a few people, I thought you were busy," says Ted.

12:58 P.M. "Staying home with the baby," says Teri.

These people are just pathetic. Their awful compulsion to celebrate hides terrible inner voids.

Maybe I'll celebrate the Chinese new year later. That's just as important. This holiday has no particular symbolism, it's a stupid ritual celebrating Christianity, it's a Newt kind of holiday, sound and fury signifying bullshit.

3:20 P.M. So Annie, Kathy, Kim are all busy elsewhere. Katya, Joe, Carlene have invited me to go to parties with them.

Who are they kidding? They only invited me because I called them, never would have even thought of me otherwise.

I make no difference in anyone's life. Everyone has someone closer to them than me.

But hey, I turned down several guys who asked me out. Okay, I didn't.

11:22 P.M. Walking the dogs, quiet, peaceful, totally obsessed with self, thinking, "This is me on New Year's Eve, so what?"

Everything seems symbolic. A homeless guy walks by with a shopping cart. I look at him, thinking, "We should commune." He scurries nervously away from me.

11:58 P.M. Everybody at my son's house greets me with hugs and kisses. This was probably a good idea. Confetti seems to be poised. Son and girlfriend inexplicably missing.

MIDNIGHT Confetti, screaming, hugs. I kiss my son's dog. My son and his girl suddenly descend the staircase, what's that on her hand?

"We're engaged!" says my little boy.

Holy shit.

Dear Problem Lady:

My best friend is also my self-appointed diet consultant. Say I'm on the phone with her, eating cashews.

"What are you eating?" she demands.

"Cashews," I answer.

"What, are you crazy? Do you know how much fat cashews contain?"

"These are dry-roasted."

"I don't care, you're consuming like three thousand calories right now!"

At first I didn't say anything because let's face it I am a bit chubby and I thought she was probably right to harangue me. But then I started losing weight. She was supportive for a while. Then one day she said, "You're not losing weight fast enough."

Now that's really wrong, isn't it? Aren't you supposed to lose weight slowly? Even if it's sometimes only two pounds a month?

So now she's at it again. And I still don't say anything, because she's basically a nice person with just as little self-esteem as I have (none) and I think if I yelled at her she'd crumble or never speak to me again.

But the compulsion to yell is growing.

Latka

Dear Latka:

It is extremely tacky for a friend to mention a friend's weight to her face. Behind her back is another thing altogether. But even if you weighed six hundred pounds and had no furniture left, a friend must not speak until spoken to. Then the floodgates may open.

You don't have to yell, however. You can do it like they tell you in magazines. Say something weasly but straightforward like, "I feel very uncomfortable and defensive when you mention my fatness and would appreciate it if you wouldn't."

Or you can tease her out of it. Tell her to do diet infomercials, that she looks more and more like Richard Simmons every day. You might even be tasteless and mention Jean Harris.

She'll get the message.

Problem Lady

Dear Problem Lady:

I would just like to say this to the world: Never, never go to your high school reunion. Ever. Because if you do you might see the guy you were in love with in eighth, ninth and tenth grades, the guy who seemed so cool, who was president of the class and who was going steady with Jeannie Cuttleburger, the most stuck-up jerk in the whole world. You might just avoid the guy all night because even after all these years your stomach may still go into knots whenever you look at him, but then he might just come up to you and ask if you remember him and you might just blurt out, "Remember you! I was madly in love with you for three years, you moron!" And he, who after twenty years may still look gorgeous, might suggest a drink. In his hotel room. And then before you know what you're doing you might be doing it. And then you might wake up the next morning, have breakfast with the guy and realize that he's a conceited ass with no sense of humor. And then you would have to go home where your beloved husband will innocently ask, "How was it, honey?" And what the hell would you say?

Oh, God, I feel so guilty! What am I going to do? I can't tell my husband what happened, he'd be really hurt. But I can't keep it to myself, my husband is my best friend and I always tell him everything. He'll understand. He'll realize that it wasn't really me in that hotel room, that my adolescent self just reared up from the past and bit me on the ass. We'll laugh about it. It will be fine.

Oh, God, why can't I bring myself to tell him?

Ramona

Dear Ramona:

You can't bring yourself to tell him because you secretly know that you can never tell him, it's not fair to cause him misery. You betrayed your husband, your penance is always keeping it to yourself.

Problem Lady

Dear Problem Lady:

I was at the drugstore the other day and this moron assistant pharmacist yelled out to the assembled masses, "Which one gets the Prozac?"

It was me. I became a man possessed. "How dare you!" I hissed furiously under my breath to the moron. "You've invaded my privacy. I want to slap you, but I won't. I'll just never come to this hellhole again." Then I flounced out, as much as a man can flounce.

Do you think I overreacted? I was so damned embarrassed, but then I wondered why. Is there a stigma against taking a lovely antidepressant? And if so, why? Should I just admit it to all and sundry? Let my Prozac out of the closet?

Willy

Dear Willy:

I was at the hairdresser's the other day and everyone there— the customers, the manicurist, the assistant, the colorist and every hairdresser—was on Prozac. It was a convention. I felt left out, the only nonmember of the club.

So I don't think it's such a big deal.

On the other hand, not everywhere is the hairdresser's.

It's a mean world, and one of the things humans most love to do is find a chink in one another's armor. So use discretion.

Problem Lady

Dear Problem Lady:

All my life I've said "heighth." I thought that's what you said. Then today my friend said to me, "It's 'height,' isn't it? At least I think so."

"Oh. Yeah, I guess it is, now that I think about it," I said casually.

"I thought so," she said.

I want to kill myself.

She knew damned well it was "height," and she finally couldn't stand it anymore.

I see the word clearly in my mind and it sure doesn't have an *h* at the end of it. I've been obsessing for ten hours now. Forty-two years, I've said "heighth." And I'm a horse trainer, can you guess how many times I've said "heighth" in my career? I'm so mortified I think I should go up to everyone I know and say, "Look, I know it's really *height,* okay? I'm not stupid or anything."

But then they'd think I was stupid *and* insane.

Should I just find a way to inject "height" into every conversation I have for the rest of my life?

Abby

Dear Abby:

You're a jock. Jocks say "heighth," even on TV, even smart jocks.

Move on.

Problem Lady

Matricidal Tendencies

Matricidal Tendencies

I love life. The way it twirls you around.

Saturday, 2 P.M., I'm wracked with self-pity. Nobody has called all day. All my so-called friends are out with their oh-so-god-damned-important significant others, even my little boy hasn't called, nobody loves me, I am way down on everyone's food chain, what's all this I keep hearing about friends being the new nuclear families, hah.

Just then the phone rings. I pounce on it, someone cares. Usually I screen calls because you never know, it could be my . . .

"Hello, dear," says a voice slurred from decades of heavy prescription-drug use.

It is! It's her! The entire reason answering machines were invented! Oh, life, you saucy, ironic playmate!

"Hello Mother." Quickly, quickly, assemble all armor, grab shields and shinguards, don flak jacket.

"I called to give you good news." My mind races, closing all ranks, slamming doors, setting alarms.

"That's nice, what good news?"

"Well (pause) I just wanted to tell you that your father is a shell of a man."

"Uh huh," I say carefully.

"The nurses say he's nothing inside, he doesn't know anyone, doesn't remember anything, he's not there anymore." Okay, duck for cover.

"So why is that good news?"

"Because you don't have to feel guilty for not visiting him."

Rat-at-at-TAT. KaBOOM. It's a magnificent hit, straight through the heart, Luke Skywalker's shot on the Death Star! My jugular is spurting. Quick, counterattack.

"So he doesn't recognize you?"

"He doesn't recognize anyone."

"Last time I was there he recognized *me*." Hah! Pow!

"Oh, well, he has his good days." Weak, very tame. Press for advantage.

"See, you have to massage his back and his neck, relax him, he's in pain, he's agitated, you need to calm him down." Take that, lousy wife and mother, daughter knows best.

Shift to another front.

"I read your new book."

"That's nice." Book came out two years ago.

"It worried me, honey, I read your book and you seemed so *depressed.*"

Depressed, am I? My enemy underestimates me. She's sending out a lure for a ten-year-old. Admit to being depressed, Mother will comfort, Mother will make it all better, unburden yourself, tell Mama. Show your weak underbelly, show Mama your throat. Say, yes, Ma, I am depressed, and here's what you'll get: Maybe dear, if you'd lose a little weight. Maybe dear, if you could get yourself a man. If you learned to cook something, try cleaning your house once in a while. Get your hair out of your face, a man might not find you so repellent. A man, a man, a man, a man! Raised to think of men as the gold ring, do feminists hate men or their mothers?

"No I'm not depressed. I'm fine." I am incredibly depressed! Nobody loves me, even you!

"I know you don't believe it, but (voice cracking) I love you very much." Now ill-concealed sobs. Crying, the age-old weapon.

"Stop that right now."

"Okay, honey, I'll stop, I'm sorry, I know you don't like me to cry."

I am a rat, I am a wretch, torturing a poor mother. My own coldness makes me feel strong, magnanimous. I make placating noises. I can be kind. After all, I am a grown-up now. I make my own way. I don't need anyone to feed me, dress me, give me a place to sleep, make me a safe world. I need to depend on nobody.

Not like my mother, who still depends on anything with a penis. I make placating noises and suddenly she is full of her new friend, Jack. Jack says this, Jack thinks that, you should meet Jack. Jack is her new talisman, her new security blanket, the old one is a shell.

Here's why we're all crazy. In the old days, fathers had all the power in the outside world, mothers had all the power in the home. Sensing a bad deal, mothers took it out on their children. But I will forgive my mother.

"I'm sure Jack is very nice," I say.

"Is it your age, honey, is that why you're so depressed? Are you sad about getting old?"

I may have to kill her.

The Chicken Goes Home to Roost

"Just brace yourself," my sister told me about our father.

I was as braced as I could get. Sick with dread, rigid with fear, but braced. I watched the bleak winter landscape of Pennsylvania whiz by, the landscape of my childhood. I felt my grown-up persona ebbing, I was more infantile by the mile.

"I am way too scared," I said to my friend Jay. My sister told me that our father's mind had just plain gone. That he would look at a cup, try to unscrew it from the table. My father is seventy-three. Doctors think he had a series of undetected strokes that atrophied his brain.

"Yeah, I'd be scared too," said Jay, who is an unreconstructed hippie version of the Rock of Gibraltar, "But it's really important to do this."

"I have to say good-bye," I said. Visions of my father were crowding my brain. When Kennedy was president everyone thought Dad looked just like him. Later he looked so much like Jimmy Carter people did triple-takes. My pharmacist dad was so tickled he would get special presidential haircuts.

"But Dad, your nose is *much* fatter," my sister and I would crow, egging him on to do his special trick. My father could make his nose skinnier at will. Without moving the rest of his face at all.

Jay and I arrived at the VA hospital to a locked floor. Old soldiers were careening through the halls—one wearing a hockey helmet and drooling, one emitting rhythmic, piercing shrieks, one doing fantastically realistic bird calls. It was a cuckoo's nest. My dad, who played airplane with me to get me to eat and always made me wear a sweater, was here somewhere. A giant guy with tattooed arms and angelic face led us to a cheery visitors' room. "I'll bring Bernie right out," he said.

Jay and I waited. I counted the chairs. I was jumping out of my skin.

And then there he was. My dad. He looked just like my dad. Walking by himself. Skinnier. My dad took one look at Jay and me and marched right out of the room. A comforting woman named Pat brought him back and said, "Your daughter's come three thousand miles to see you, Bernie, don't you want to visit with her?" My dad looked terrified and refused all eye contact.

"Hiya Dad," I said, "I'm glad to see you." My dad. Always harassed and busy, always trying to pay off a new house, another sports car, always dressed in ultimate tweediness with a full head of presidential hair, now in sweatpants and tie-dyed shirt, hair shorn, blue eyes enormous behind magnification glasses. He turned his face away. I got right into it and stayed there, making his eyes look at me.

"Doncha remember your daughter, Bernie?" asked Pat. I stayed in his face. Finally his blue eyes locked with mine and he smiled. "Now I do," he said. I tried to hug him. He remained rigid. Then he sat down and took his shoes right off. He didn't remember Jay and was afraid to look at him.

"Do you like it here, Dad?"

"I would, but I've got to go down to the borok and catch that thing before it teecox lembo . . ." He drifted off and his face became fixed.

"Are you happy or unhappy?"

"Unhappy. I've got to check the time, it's late, the guys are all off flaging gollar . . ."

I looked at Jay, he patted my hand. Tears were streaming down my face. I kept up the chatter. "Remember Chipper?"

"Now there's a good dog, he was here today." My beloved schnauzer Chipper died in 1970. For a fleeting second I envied my dad his time with Chipper. But no. The man was so agitated. It didn't matter that all his sentences trailed into gibberish, he had to get somewhere, he had to do something, he had to save everyone, he was late, he was needed, he was responsible.

When dad first started going strange, his young second wife just split. He was alone and terrified, he knew what was happening to him, but he couldn't call us, his daughters were his responsibility, not vice versa. Finally he turned up on my mother's doorstep, "just to say hello." He went downhill fast after that.

I kept saying, "Daddy, it's okay, you can relax, we're all okay, you don't have to worry. We're *fine*." That is what becomes of too many men. They spend their lives shouldering the entire burden of financial care of their families. Even their wives become glorified children. So now, after even rational thought is gone, my father is still the essence of anxiety and responsibility.

I fed him. "Here comes the airplane!" I said, and he opened his mouth like a baby bird. Eventually he took the spoon and started shoveling in chicken and noodles, applesauce. Jay and I noticed that when we talked to each other, Dad relaxed. He liked being out of the action.

An old guy waltzed into the room, bellowing, "Donna! Donna!"

Pat pulled him away. "Joe, your daughter is fine and living in New York."

"Then how come she's dead?" Joe asked plaintively.

Pat ruffled Dad's hair and kissed his cheek. He kissed her right back.

I gave him a neck and back massage. He visibly relaxed. He started calling me honey and baby and telling me how beautiful I was, the only way my dad knew to compliment his girls. "How's your sister?" he even asked. His speech had reduced to familiar endearments, but the emotions were alive and kicking. So it wasn't good-bye at all. We were closer than we'd been since the chasm of my teenhood opened up and had us fighting constantly for the control of my life.

What if my mother had been a stronger woman? Even a feminist? What if she had worked? Taken on at least part of his lonely burdens? Would he have had those tiny tragic strokes?

I hugged him and kissed him good-bye, he hugged and kissed me back. Then he summoned up his manly civility to say to Jay, "It was good to see you. I'm sorry I didn't remember you before." And to me: "Take care of yourself, baby."

Fathers and Daughters: A Pop Quiz

*F*our of my close friends are pregnant. All of them are having girls. Extrapolating outward, this clearly means that 30 percent of women of childbearing age are at this very moment pregnant with girls. And the burning question is: Will these innocent tiny fetuses grow up to become young women every bit as confused and fucked up as my friends and I?

I do not want to see our future women awash with neuroses, low self-esteem and double messages. To curtail this eventuality, I have prepared a little quiz you can all take to see if you'd make a good dad. Go ahead, make my day.

1. Every time I turn on a talk show or read a book or newspaper, the topic of incest/child abuse smacks me in the face. Although I had no idea that incest/child abuse is our new national pastime, my own feelings about it are:

    a. A man feeds and clothes and cares for his children and they owe him something. They owe him everything. They are *his* children and whatever he chooses to do with them is his business.

b. I was beat up and abused regularly by my own father and I hate him for it. I am a boiling cauldron of rage. I hope to God I don't do anything like that to my own children. I'm kind of pretty sure I won't.
c. Some kids are always flaunting themselves in front of you, they're just asking for it.
d. It's not so bad if it's a niece or second cousin or something.

Yup, that was a trick question designed to weed out the psychos amongst you. If you even contemplated a, b, c, or d, you are never allowed to be a father. Immediately begin ten years of intensive psychotherapy or shoot yourself.

2. I have heard that a child's self-image is initially (and usually indelibly) shaped by her parents' feedback. My daughter is pretty, good in math, scared of riding her bike, always climbing trees, and obsessed with weird, punk clothing. To give her a positive self-image
a. I would tell her she is beautiful, gorgeous, a real knockout, a heartbreaker.
b. I would work with her every day to help her learn to ride her bike.
c. Every time she got an A in math I'd give her a special treat.
d. I'd tell her she cannot climb trees unless with a grown-up, I'd play math games with her, I'd let the bike rust, I'd give her a specified clothing allowance and let her wear whatever the hell she wants.

If you answered a, you're doing what countless fathers before you have done: You've focused on your daughter's appearance instead of her intrinsic self-worth. She will become crazed about her looks and let her inner self atrophy. If she grows up to be plain, she will feel worthless. If she grows up to be pretty, she will constantly need reassurance yet still feel worthless. If she grows up to be Brigitte Bardot reincarnated, she will become an arrogant, spoiled, man-teaser who will revel in her stunningness until her looks start to fade, when she will try to kill herself.

If you answered b, you're ignoring all her positive aspects and rubbing her nose in her weakness. She will grow up lacking confidence, always sure that whatever she does well is not nearly as important as her failures. Plan on plenty of therapy bills.

If you answered c, you're a lousy party-pooper. Before you know it, she'll stop having fun with math and start feeling pressured to please you. Let her have her own successes and enjoy them with her, let her have her failures and commiserate with her. Don't be Bob Barker.

If you answered d, you're a fab parent. You know that children need reasonable limits to feel safe and loved, you know that if you let her climb trees unsupervised she'd think, "Jeez, they really want to get rid of me." Letting her wear whatever she wants tells her no matter how weird she is, you love her anyway. And children, trust me, usually think they are incredibly weird.

3. My daughter is leaving for summer camp tomorrow. I want her to go out to dinner with the family. She wants to spend her last night with her friends. My response is
   a. "You'll have dinner with us, young lady, and like it."
   b. "I can't believe, after all your mother and I have done for you, that you don't want to be with us."
   c. "Honey, are you sure I can't guilt-trip you into being with us?"
   d. "Oh, who cares what the hell you do?"

If you answered a, you'll be doing a perfectly fine parent thing. She'll be miserable and hate you all through dinner, and then be really thrilled to get away from you the next day.

If you answered b, you're causing more trouble than you can even imagine. One of the most difficult issues of childhood is separating from one's parents. By guilt-tripping her, she'll not only be afraid of leaving

*you for her own sake, but now you've given her the added burden of
your happiness. She'll feel she is destroying you by leaving and will end
up a bitter and twisted human, either running away when she is sixteen or living at home until she is fifty.*

*If you answered c, you are a gifted parent. You are not only ac-
knowledging that you are in a position to misuse your power over your
child, you are showing that you have weakness, and are therefore not
God. You're making a joke about the serious problem of separation and
becoming your kid's ally instead of her enemy. Someday I hope to be
just like you.*

*If you answered d, your kid, with everykid's fragile ego, will be-
lieve you. Is that what you want?*

4. Wait a minute, I don't have space for question four. This column has run totally away with me. Okay, just some final words:
Don't ever use the word "ladylike." Don't ever say, "Only boys can
do that." Don't encourage your boys to be strong and assertive and
your daughters to be meek and submissive. And whatever you do,
do not take your child to cocktail parties and force everyone to
make a great big fuss.

Intimacy with Vomit

I had a perfectly lovely pregnancy. I was never sick. I thought everything that happened to my body was too fascinating and fabulous. The whole thing was a snap. I was twenty years old.

That was twenty-three years ago. Now all of my friends are pregnant at once. The youngest is thirty-seven, the oldest is forty-three. They're all utterly insane.

"I had hot chocolate today," said Cleo, "and when I threw it up and flushed the toilet, the powder that you make the hot chocolate from was in the toilet. Hot chocolate goes right back to its original elements."

"I can't believe you didn't tell me Cleo was pregnant," said Nora. "I don't give a flying fuck that she made you swear not to! It's inexcusable! *And* she's a month further along than me. *And* she's having her amnio today and I have to wait a month. What is this, some kind of conspiracy?"

"You know who I really hate?" asked Jane. "Pregnant women who take aerobics classes. No! Here's who I hate more. There was a woman in an elevator, clearly ready to give birth, and she says to her husband, 'Do you want to go home or go look at some suits?'

Look at some suits? I can't even dress myself and she's looking at
suits?"

The guys don't know what hit them.

Brendan, who always has to know everything, pretends he has
it covered. "Whatever Cleo wants, I just do it instantly," he said.
"It's not hard, all you have to do is move up from being a guy to
being a fundamentally decent human being, and you get fucking
Nobel credit. You just take every particle of contrariness out of
your brain.

"There's nothing rational about this, from her wanting the
fucking pickles and ice cream, to her not being able to stand the
smell of the fucking paint that's been on the same wall for nine
years, to puking her guts out for no reason."

"He hugs me while I'm throwing up and tells me I'm a hero,"
says Cleo. "He lets me describe my vomit to him without getting
sick."

Whereas Nora has Eli flummoxed. "Every time I work up an
appetite she mentions her vaginal discharge. She feels compelled to
describe the different varieties. The word 'gelatinous' was never
heard in our household before she developed her condition.

"And you know what gets me? She's gained, like, a pound
and a half . . ."

"Five pounds!" Nora shrieked from the other room.

"Right," he said. "She walks around the apartment with both
hands rubbing her belly. And then she needs two canes. Like Dr.
Johnson. There are Mexican and Chinese women in their eighth
month of pregnancy working in sweatshops all day, meanwhile this
girl has gained a pound and a half and needs two canes.

"Today's big thing was that they discovered a polyp on her
cervix. She called me, crying, hysterical. So what are the big impli-
cations? Turns out we can't have sex. 'Well, maybe I can give you a
handjob,' she said. I'm going to hang a sign on her that says OUT OF
ORDER."

"What about the smell thing?" I asked.

"What smell thing?" he wondered.

He doesn't know how lucky he is.

"Any kind of meat smell, I'm outta here," said Cleo. "I have the sense of smell of a dog. I can smell people's skin. Anything clean, get it over here and I'm sticking it up my nose. I love the smell of water, it's like amniotic fluid. I'm feeling like part of the Earth. We're just like animals when we're pregnant. Brendan smells like the nectar of the gods. Which must be nature's way of saying he's my man. Except if he's had garlic. Then he makes me puke."

"If Al has had garlic within the week I can't go near him," said Jane. "Today I drove into Hollywood and there was a skunk smell. I could barely drive home. Then I retched and retched until I thought my teeth would fall out."

Which brings us, backwards, to food.

"You gotta make sure that the three or four things they can eat are always available," said Al. "She can't go into the kitchen, the smell makes her vomit, so I do all the cooking of the narrow band of things she can tolerate. Last week it was bonito sashimi, which is a small tuna that swims only twice a year. You try finding that at the drop of a hat. Basil can cause a miscarriage, which was not a problem in your day. Who ate basil? But now you're all sophisticated.

"This week it's easy, turkey sandwiches. But sliced just to a certain thickness, with a very specific amount of mayonnaise. I had to have her demonstrate it to me. I took Polaroids."

"We drive all the way out to Brooklyn because she must have a steak and when we get there she gets an individual can of tuna," said Eli.

"He takes me to the supermarket and we buy whatever I think I might keep down. I'm like a dog sniffing for drugs," said Cleo.

Then there are the extraterrestrial mood swings.

"We had to go to this genetic counselor. I thought it would

just be technical," said Eli. "But this woman is a social worker. She makes the huge mistake of asking Nora, 'How do you feel about this pregnancy?' Next thing I'm surrounded by two women sobbing and talking about their relationship with their mothers."

"They're like the weather," said Brendan. "Beyond unpredictable. Just some swirling shit on a map. Nothing you can do anything about."

"First it's anger and yelling, then it's tears, then every once in a while happiness in the face of everything," said Al. "It's like 'Oh! The Joker's here today.' "

"Have you thought about how hard it is for her?" I asked.

"Yeah, right," he said. "Exactly what they said about the Germans. I'm joining the men's liberation army."

Just wait till they get to the actual birth.

Dear Problem Lady:

Don't you think that as women get older they automatically get weird?

I thought it was just my mother, who is now completely loopy. She has to know everything that's going on, even if it has to do with a second cousin twice removed and why he got his pay docked one day last week. Plus she must have a say in everything to the point where she is talking back to Tom Brokaw. She used to just dote on Tom, but now she has to contradict everything he says and complain about his New Jersey accent, like he can hear her.

Worst of all, she has to pretend she knows best even though she doesn't know shit. We went to England last year, where I have been dozens of times and she never. But she had to point to every truck and say, "That's a lorry, you know." In London she was constantly stopping "the nice bobbies." She insisted that the Lake District was always awash with rain because the cashier at Woolworth's brother-in-law Lou is the world's expert on the Lake District.

As it turned out, it *was* pissing with rain in the Lake District. You can only imagine how she gloated. I finally just left her in a "darling tea shoppe" and strode around muttering for hours and ended up with bronchitis.

I'd been suffering quietly and thinking, "Why? Why my mother? Why me?" when I started hearing from my friends that their mothers were also bonkers. In exactly the same way! The noses stuck in everything, the insistence on omniscience!

We're all in our early forties, our mothers are mid- to late sixties. Is this a disease? Could we start a support group for children of diseased mothers?

Marion

Dear Marion:

What you're describing in your mother is an enormous need for control. I wonder why.

Could it have anything to do with the forces around her? Like the fact that when she goes to get some milk the deli guy is flirting with a teenager and literally doesn't see her? And that when she finally speaks up the deli guy and the teenager roll their eyes as if she's the biggest nuisance on the planet?

Could it have anything to do with that jeans commercial where a woman her age is shown not only to be the enemy, but ridiculous for finding young people in their hip clothes revolting?

How about the fact that whenever she sees a movie where a woman her age is portrayed as sexual, it's simply a device for thigh-slapping comic relief?

Your mother is constantly being smashed in the face with the fact that she is not only useless but invisible, and when she's not invisible she's ridiculous.

Do you think that may have something to do with her over-whelming desire for control, her grasping at any straw to be noticed and listened to?

Come on Marion, who really needs the support group here?

Problem Lady

Dear Problem Lady:

My friend, or kind of a friend anyway, well I guess she's my friend, anyway she's in the hospital. And I have her dog.

It's been three months now. Susie, who's been in a wheelchair for seventeen years, suddenly woke up really sick and next thing we all knew she was in the hospital with a bone infection and nobody could take her dog, they all have too many and I only have one so I said I would.

This dog Barkley is a handful. He jumps up on the sofas, he digs holes in the garden, he even figured out how to open the refrigerator and stole my dinner a couple of times. I always know when he's done it because he hides under the dining room table like I can't see him.

Anyway, my dog, Sasha, is used to having me to herself. Every time Barkley comes up to me, Sasha pushes him out of the way. Sasha sleeps on the bed so Barkley thinks he should too.

Meanwhile I just got a call from Susie and she's really freaked out because the doctor was saying they may have to amputate a leg. She could be in the hospital forever.

I know I sound cold, but I'm tired of taking care of Barkley. Things are awful for Susie, but she's an adult, isn't she? She's responsible for her own life, even if it sucks. Nobody who's a grown-up can expect someone else to pick up the slack for her forever.

Don't you think, even if it seems a little creepy, that I have the right to phone Susie and tell her she's got to make other arrangements?

Beth

Dear Beth:

Nobody is a grown-up. Especially someone incredibly ill in the hospital. Don't you even try to shift the blame from yourself.

People don't live within families anymore. Who can blame them, what with Dad being a distant figure, Mom being an alcoholic, and Uncle Al being a child abuser? So we're all isolated, unless we live in New Guinea or somewhere where they still have hunter-gatherer societies whose families pick up the slack from each other without a blink and never have to join Al-Anon.

Friends are the twenty-first-century version of extended families. Friends nurture each other, take on each other's responsibilities. This is a commitment, not something you turn on and off like a tap.

You are a selfish whiner. If you keep it up, not too far in the future you will be lonely, isolated, and muttering to yourself in restaurants about how nothing's your fault. Nobody will care.

Barkley is behaving in normal dog mode. You're lucky he's not acting insanely, since his heart is probably broken. If you don't want to deal with him anymore, *you* make the arrangements. And you'd better find someplace good enough, someplace where you would put your beloved Sasha if you had to, or karmic law will decree that you come back as a dog. In China.

Problem Lady